It is simply

A Matter
Of When

John Palmer

Copyright © 2020 by John Palmer. All rights reserved.
Except for brief excerpts for review purposes,
no part of this book may be reproduced or used in any form
without written permission from the author.

John Palmer
amatterofwhen@yahoo.com

Unless otherwise indicated, all Scripture quotations are from the
ESV Bible (The Holy Bible, English Standard Version), copyright 2001
by Crossway, a publishing ministry of Good News Publishers.
Used by permission. All rights reserved.

Scripture quotations marked *(NIV)* are taken from *the Holy Bible,
New International Version*®, *NIV*®. Copyright © 1973, 1978, 1984,
2011
by Biblica, Inc.™ Used by permission of Zondervan. All rights reserved
worldwide.

Emphasis in Scripture quotations added by author.

ISBN: 978-1-950873-99-9

TABLE OF CONTENTS

PREFACE: A Wee Word of Introduction 1

CHAPTER 1: Starting with the Correct Mindset
Believe It or Not, It Is Coming 3

CHAPTER 2: Choosing the Right Method of Interpretation
Understanding God's Intent 17

CHAPTER 3: On the Road to the Olivet Discourse
(*Matthew 21:42*) The Stone the Builders Rejected ... 25

CHAPTER 4: The Olivet Discourse, Part 1
(*Matthew 24:1–14*) Not as Complicated as You Might Think 35

CHAPTER 5: The Olivet Discourse, Part 2
(*Matthew 24:15–31*) Not as Easy as We Would Like 43

CHAPTER 6: The Olivet Discourse, Part 3
(*Matthew 24:32–51*) Those That Believe Are Prayerfully Watching 63

CHAPTER 7: The Olivet Discourse, Part 4
(*Matthew 25:1–13; Parable of the Ten Virgins*)
Do You Have Enough Oil? 79

CHAPTER 8: The Olivet Discourse, Part 5
(*Matthew 25:18–30; Parable of the Talents*)
Have You Invested Wisely? 87

CHAPTER 9: The Olivet Discourse, Part 6
(*Matthew 25:31–46; Sheep and the Goats*)
Have You Done the Master's Will or Your Own?... 97

CHAPTER 10: The Seventy Weeks of Daniel, Part 1
(*Daniel 9:1–26a*) Do You Know and Understand? ...107

CHAPTER 11: The Seventy Weeks of Daniel, Part 2
(*Daniel 9:26b–27*) Are You Ready for the "Ruler" and the Final Week of Current World History?... 121

CHAPTER 12: The Final Vision of Daniel
(*Daniel chapters 10–12*) Those Who Are Wise Shall Understand... 135

CHAPTER 13: The Mountain of the Lord, a Thousand-Year Reign, and the New Heavens and New Earth
The Things the Lord Has Prepared for Those Who Love Him—But Are They Literal or Symbolic?.... 153

Preface

A Wee Word of Introduction

Suppose you were told that a major catastrophe was looming on the horizon, and the source is highly credible. You also hear it is possible to receive advance warning that may not only help you save loved ones but countless others from horrific disaster, pain, and hardship. Would you want to know more? Most would say, "Of course!" If this is also your reaction, then read on.

Once the apocalyptic winds of change begin to envelop the four corners of Earth, revealing signs the Bible states will be clearly recognizable to all who are intently watching, a growing number of people believe we will have very little time to make any final preparations ahead of the storm that is predicted to encompass the entire world. The change they are talking about is the kind that will forever alter our planet and bring about the end of world history as we know it.

In their opinion it is not a matter of if, just a matter of when.

If they are correct, will you be ready? They say you could be, that you should be, and that if you knew what was coming, you would absolutely want to be. They would tell you, "This is for you and for those you love, for all you can hopefully influence for good along the way."

For them, this kind of knowledge is truly a once-in-a-lifetime opportunity, one not to pass up, one you will be glad you did not.

Are they right? You must decide for yourself.

IT IS SIMPLY A MATTER OF WHEN

Chapter 1

Starting with the Correct Mindset

Believe It or Not, It Is Coming

Imagine
You get an emergency call at work. Local authorities inform you that your house was suddenly engulfed in flames because of a freak lightning strike. Thankfully nobody was in the house, but nothing is left. Everything was destroyed. Like a thief in the night, circumstances beyond your control have robbed you of your home and its contents. No warning. No way to prepare. In a matter of minutes, it is all gone.

In the past decade alone we have either seen on the news or have personally witnessed someone being displaced from their residence by any number of tragic events. Disasters like fire, flood, mudslide, tornado, hurricane, typhoon, nor'easter, tsunami, earthquake, war—and even global pandemic—are ever before us. Apart from rare exceptions, no one in any of these circumstances is adequately prepared. Hundreds of thousands worldwide have had to face one or more of these gut-wrenching situations that only too often include the loss of loved ones. If it were not for the many relief organizations and governmental efforts to support those who are caught in the midst of such devastation, there would be no aid or recourse for anyone. Yet even with help, the rebuilding process is arduous at best. Some people never fully recover. Many receive nothing at all.

More alarming than the above is what the world will apparently experience during the final years leading up to Jesus' return to Earth. According to His own words, those Jesus Himself relayed to His disciples on the Mount of Olives outside Jerusalem just prior to His betrayal and crucifixion, the aforementioned catastrophes will pale in comparison to the events that will unfold preceding His arrival, *"For then there will be **great tribulation**, such as has not been from the beginning of the world until now, no, and never will be"* (Matthew 24:21, emphasis added).

The Bible states that *the day of the Lord*, one of the major end-time events surrounding Jesus' second coming during these *latter days*, will light upon the world like *a thief in the night* (1 Thessalonians 5:2). Not only will it take most of the world by surprise, it will initiate unimaginable consternation on Earth.

When we read such stories in the Bible, especially the ones dealing with seemingly terrifying events like some of those described in the book of Revelation, we naturally tend to set them aside. They either invoke a sense of overwhelming fear or we simply do not understand. But if you are a follower of Jesus, you need to understand. And after reading this book you will hopefully want to understand. When the countdown of the last years of current world history commences, you should already have a keen awareness, and a knowledgeable understanding, of all that is taking place.

As startling as all of this may seem, there is encouraging news. You will see, as each piece of the puzzle is revealed and set in place, that the hand of God is in control of every facet of the end times. We have nothing to fear if we pay close attention to how we should prepare. In fact, for those who follow Jesus, this is the most exciting time in our history. The Lord's second coming ushers in His rule and reign on Earth forever. You will not be able to change what is written in Scripture, but you can be ready so that *you are not in darkness, brothers, for that day to surprise you like a thief* (1 Thessalonians 5:4).

I have endeavored to make the reading of this book, and any continuing research on your own, as easy and simple as possible. I hope to give you a basic foundation upon which you can construct your own biblical understanding of end-time events. But as with any study like this, it is not without controversy and challenges.

THE CONTROVERSY

There are nearly as many differences of opinion concerning how these end-time events will actually unfold as there are Christian denominations. Opinions on the subject are often passionate, and conversations can easily become heated. For this reason, many well-meaning Christians simply shy away from the subject altogether, pastors and preachers included.

Let me share with you one such experience.

I was once invited to lead a men's Bible study group at a church I was visiting in Ohio. I had just returned to the U.S. after thirteen years of missionary work in South America. As would be expected, many people in the congregation were eager to hear about my experiences. Though the leader of the group made no direct request, it later became apparent that he was hoping I would recount some exciting stories of my years overseas.

It is Simply A Matter Of When

He finally approached me a few days before the meeting and, anxious to know the topic, asked if I had decided what to share with the men. I said I was considering discussing a couple of chapters from the book of Matthew. Somewhat surprised, he asked, "Which ones?" Sensing that divulging the subject matter might be met with a bit of reservation, I calmly replied, in matter-of-fact fashion, "Why Matthew chapters 24 and 25." What followed came as no surprise.

These two chapters in Matthew carry a very familiar and important message, yet one that is also full of controversy. They are familiar because they contain the most detailed account of what Jesus told His disciples about the events surrounding His second coming and the end of life on Earth as we know it. They are important because they present a sequential outline of events leading up to His return to Earth and what will transpire during these times. They can also be highly controversial, as various assumptions are made about these chapters to prove any number of divergent theological positions. Depending on one's viewpoint, interpretations of key verses in Matthew chapters 24 and 25 can result in some interesting twists and turns—and spark intense debate.

The group leader mentioned to the pastor of the hosting church my topic of choice for the upcoming men's meeting and voiced his concern. As a result, the pastor decided to attend the study himself to hear what I had to say. I fully appreciated the pastor's desire to protect his flock. Anyone with a shepherd's heart would do the same. However, I felt an inner peace about the subject matter as I planned on using an approach that would probably be different from anything they had ever experienced.

It became obvious, as each of the men entered the church classroom on the night of the meeting, that most of them had already been told the topic of discussion. Though the men were quite cordial—pastor included—there was a noticeable air of apprehension. If necessary, each man seemed ready to defend his position.

Understanding the situation at hand, I asked if I could begin with a word of prayer.

"Heavenly Father, I thank You for all these men who are willing to take time out from their busy lives and schedules to gather around Your Word. There are many ways we can approach Your Word, but there is only one that is most pleasing to you. Help us, Father, to find this way as we read Your Word with an open heart and an open mind. Our desire is to see Your Word the way You intend it to be seen. We pray that Your will, rather than ours, would be done this evening. Amen."

An anxious silence filled the room, so I dove right in.

"There are many interpretations of end-time events described in the Bible. Two of the most debated concern the timing of Jesus' second coming and what is commonly referred to as the rapture or miraculous ascent of the saints living on Earth into the heavens. For those who believe that this rapture will occur near a period of **great tribulation**, two opposing positions tend to take center stage.

"The most popular, which we will call the pre-tribulation position, proposes that Jesus' true church, those of His followers living on Earth during the time of His second coming, will be taken up by Him in a rapture-like resurrection before any serious *tribulation* befalls Earth at the time of the end.

"A generally less popular belief, which we will call the post-tribulation position, suggests that the church will pass through a severe time of testing during this *tribulation* period prior to Jesus' return. They believe that after the *tribulation*, as opposed to before, He will rapture the surviving saints on Earth to be with Him in the heavenly realms.

"Among mainstream Christian scholars, there are differing opinions surrounding these two positions, but a significant number of them fall within the framework of one or the other.

"Such extreme differences understandably spawn spirited conversation, with each side laboring intensely to prove they are correct. However, what any of us personally believes to be true is frankly irrelevant. Only what God wants us to understand, as stated in His Word, is what matters. And there is hardly a better place to begin an end-time study than with what Jesus personally states about His own return. So, rather than debate the various positions, I thought it would be more beneficial if we just read directly from Matthew chapters 24 and 25. They contain the most detailed account of Jesus' earthly discourse on these events. Simply listen to what He has to say. Maybe we can go around the room with each reading one verse at a time. My only hope is that we do so with an open heart and an open mind."

What happened at this point was extraordinary. The initial atmosphere of tense anticipation suddenly turned to one of curious reservation. As each man read his verse in succession, an almost mitigating calm descended upon the group one by one. We read straight through these two chapters in a slow but steady rhythm. Not a single commentary was offered—not by me, the pastor, or anyone else. God's Word was speaking directly to the heart and mind of each man.

When we finished reading, there was a deafening silence. (Fifteen seconds can seem like an eternity in such situations.) I finally spoke up.

"I am not going to tell you what I believe about what we just read, as it is not important for our discussion here. What is important is that we each seek to understand God's message to us as revealed in His Word. But as food for thought, let us take a step back and look at the potential ramifications of adhering specifically to either of the opposing positions I mentioned earlier and what the effect might be on us, our loved ones, and the church.

"Suppose you subscribe to some form of the pre-tribulation stance. You believe that Jesus will come to rapture His church before any major *tribulation* envelops Earth. According to this position, Jesus comes, He raptures His church, and—all jesting aside—who is the happy camper? You? Absolutely! What you believed has come to pass and you will be with Jesus forever, far away from the turmoil on Earth below. But what about those that subscribe to the post-tribulation position who thought they had to pass through a period of **great tribulation** before being raptured by Jesus? Will they be happy? Of course! Why not? Some of their end-time doctrine might have been wrong, and their positioning of the rapture might have been misplaced within the overall sequence of events, yet none of this matters anymore. They were prepared for the worst but are now safe with Jesus along with you. In the end, it seems like a win/win for everyone!

"Now let us look at those subscribing to the post-tribulation position. They generally believe that the world will suddenly be tossed into a major *tribulation* period, a time more cataclysmic than anything ever witnessed on Earth prior to Jesus' return, the rapture of the church, and the impending wrath of God. For them, this perilous time is acutely described in Matthew chapter 24, and they think that the church will be plunged directly into it.

"Now what if? What if this interpretation is, in fact, the actual order of events? Those that hold to this position will have kept a close eye on the relevant signs of the times they see described in the Bible so that they can be as prepared as possible for the onslaught of the **great tribulation**. Some of them might develop discreet places of refuge for themselves, their loved ones, and other believers. A few might feel called to remain and be a witness, even if it means dying as a martyr. There are many different paths that they might take, but they will already have been counting the cost and preparing to face the upheaval they anticipate.

"If what they foresee actually comes to pass, will they be happy? Although happy might not be the best word to use here, the answer is still—as far as they are concerned—absolutely yes. Why? They believe that once the **great tribulation** begins, as predicted by specific signs they see detailed in the Bible, the days are numbered before the church will be gathered together by Jesus into the heavenly realms to be with Him forever. Although they understand that this *tribulation* period will accompany extreme challenges, through these hardships and difficulties they will have an inner sense of relief and joy knowing that the end is coming soon.

"Let us pause for a moment and take a serious look at this.

"If you hold to the pre-tribulation position, would you have the same inner peace in this scenario? Not likely. Unless you are familiar with post-tribulation doctrine, you would be far from prepared. You would have virtually no clue as to what is actually going on. You would suddenly find yourself in the midst of the greatest crisis the world has ever seen, and without direction. You would likely be totally confused—and lost—with a myriad of conflicting thoughts racing through your mind.

"How does the saying go? 'It is better to have and not need than to need and not have.' If the church, or saints, are all taken up by Jesus in some sort of rapture before the **great tribulation**—this ominous period described by Jesus in Matthew chapter 24—then all true believers will rejoice together. But if the destiny of the church is to pass through this forewarned period of *tribulation* to be purified before any rapture at Jesus' coming, an overwhelming number of Christians will be caught by surprise and totally unprepared.

"What if? It is a question worth seriously considering. You might want to read over these chapters in Matthew again on your own as you carefully consider the position you currently hold. Hopefully we are prepared for whatever may possibly transpire within our lifetime or the next few generations.

"What if?"

After a final prayer, the meeting was over. The mood was somber, yet there was a quiet sense of renewed awareness in the air. I shook hands with the men as they filed out of the room. The comments from each of them, though brief, seemed to echo the ones before: "This certainly has me thinking. I need to go back and read these chapters again."

Waiting to be the last to leave, the pastor shook my hand and said, "You know, there have been many folks come to this church to speak about the end times, and it has almost always left the congregation sideways. For this reason, I finally adopted a policy to avoid the subject with the congregation altogether. Then when I was told what you were going to discuss at this study tonight I thought, 'Uh-oh, not another one!' But this was very different. I needed this. We all needed this. To continue avoiding the subject because it is controversial is an affront to God and a major neglect of one of the most important events in His Word. I learned something this evening. I also have some reading to do. I need to follow up on what was started today."

The Bible states that *"no prophecy of Scripture comes from someone's own interpretation. For no prophecy was ever pro-*

It is Simply A Matter Of When

duced by the will of man; but men spoke from God as they were carried along by the Holy Spirit" (2 Peter 1:20–21). This raises an extremely important question: If the Bible outlines what will transpire during the end times, and there are highly educated scholars poring over this material, then why is there such a vast array of opinion on how it will unfold?

Much of the controversy surrounding the topic of end-time events can be avoided if we would honestly just listen to what God's Word says apart from our personal biases. Only too often have those with the best of intentions endeavored to use the Scriptures to confirm their own notions or ideas instead of simply allowing Scripture to speak for itself. But there is more at play here than mere human prejudice.

Satan, the devourer (1 Peter 5:8), is very much alive and present in our world. He longs for incessant controversy and confusion about the Bible. He certainly wants no one to understand the end times. As far as he is concerned, the less anyone knows about the last days, the more people he can destroy—anyone who is not prepared. Satan works relentlessly to alienate, divide, and conquer—and to keep as many as possible away from the truth. How does he do it? How has he succeeded in dividing some of the greatest Christian scholars over this topic for the past two millennia, and how can we avoid this happening to us? The answer is simple: knowing Satan's devices, and how he works, can help us overcome his deceitful and perfidious tactics (2 Corinthians 2:11).

Believe it or not, many people believe what they believe simply because they have been taught by someone to believe it. (Repetition intended.) For those of you who hold to a particular biblical doctrine, your teaching may have come from an individual, a denominational school, a church, the reading of a Bible-based commentary, a novel, or even a movie. If you are part of an organization that requires strict adherence to approved theology, you often run the risk of being asked to leave their fellowship if you question core beliefs.

Scholarly teaching is usually well presented and very convincing. Therefore, you might reason, if the doctrine you are acquainted with seems to make sense—and nothing blatant sticks out that would cause you to question it—why rock the boat? After all, your family and close friends have accepted it for eons! But what if later you want to take a closer look at what you believe and become a more knowledgeable student of the Bible yourself? What if you begin to see things differently, even some important things? There is still the struggle of adhering to the accepted beliefs of your particular organization to remain a member. This makes questioning their doctrine a touchy subject, and why many people tend to stick with what they have been taught. Yet there is one major problem with taking this stance, or blindly accepting someone else's theological inclination: what you have been told, or asked to believe, might be wrong—even deadly wrong.

We each have mental filters through which we process all information. These filters come from belief systems we have adopted and developed over the years. Some filters are easily modified while others require a major paradigm shift to be transformed. For those of us with our own ideas about the end times, it is no different. This is where I caution you. It is irrelevant what any of us thinks or wants to believe. The only thing that matters is what God's Word states. This may seem obvious enough, but beware. If the doctrinal filters we use to develop our theology are wrong our conclusions will be wrong as well.

In order to correctly understand end-time events, or any other subject in the Bible, we must begin with the right mindset. Though there are numerous end-time theological ideologies, only one of them is going to be the most accurate. Choosing the best one will probably depend on whether or not we have successfully eliminated all harmful filters within our hearts and minds that may cloud the truth. When dealing with an issue of such tremendous magnitude as this, coming to the wrong conclusion could be very costly to us and others. Hence, one of the initial purposes of this book is to challenge and inform both our mindset and our understanding of Scripture. We also need to clearly define the ground rules for interpreting the Bible. This will help eliminate any filters that may cause us to err from correctly interpreting God's Word.

THE CHALLENGE

Before diving into our study, let us begin with what this book is not meant to be, which is a tell-all, answer-all, exhaustive guide concerning biblical end-time events.

We will not explore all the varying thoughts and opinions on each subject, and this book does not contain footnotes, a glossary, or a lengthy bibliography. Such a comprehensive work would take volumes to complete, and this is not a doctoral dissertation. This is a simple man's approach to what is often considered a subject too complicated for the average person—like me—or that of Jesus' original disciples, some of whom were considered *uneducated, common men* (Acts 4:13).

The main goal of this book is to help anyone, professing Christian or not, begin to take a serious look at end-time events using the best source for it: the Bible.

Please do not misinterpret my intention here. There is a definite inclination of thought outlined in this study, and I believe you will find it quite compelling. Nonetheless, my sincere hope is that you will not simply accept my direction and guidance no matter how convincing it might seem. I would encourage you to not blindly take anyone's teaching as "the gospel truth" about this or any other biblical subject. Open the Bible with me and read the same verses as we study this together. My desire is to get you moving in the right direction, to inspire you to search out the truth in God's Word for yourself, just like the Bereans during the time of the apostle Paul.

Now the Berean Jews were of more noble character than those in Thessalonica, for they received the message with great eagerness and examined the Scriptures every day to see if what Paul said was true (Acts 17:11 NIV).

The apostle Paul wisely instructed his young disciple Timothy in a similar manner:

Do your best to present yourself to God as one approved, a worker who has no need to be ashamed, rightly handling the word of truth (2 Timothy 2:15).

When it comes to understanding the latter days, personal study is crucial. You will find phrases such as *"He who has ears to hear, let him hear"* used by Jesus various times in the New Testament (Matthew 11:15; Mark 4:9, 23; Luke 8:8, 14:35). However, Jesus' phrase *"let the reader understand"* is recorded only once during what is called the **Olivet Discourse** when He explains to His disciples the events that surround His return to Earth (Matthew 24:15, Mark 13:14; emphasis added). This is significant. By instructing His disciples to go back and research the relevant passages in the book of Daniel, Jesus knew that His discourse on the Mount of Olives, coupled with these writings of Daniel, would enlighten not only them but countless others yet to come. He knew we would all discover important additional information in the book of Daniel about the time of His return, details we would not want to miss.

The Olivet Discourse, as recounted in the book of Matthew, will be the centerpiece of our study. What better place to begin formulating our end-time doctrine than with the words of Jesus Himself as He describes to His disciples the events that encompass His second coming? After journeying through the Olivet Discourse, we will take a brief look at the related passages Jesus makes reference to in the book of Daniel.

As stated earlier, this book is meant to aid you in your ongoing personal research. Your job will be to read through this material, verify the information presented by using the best method of interpretation—which we will introduce next—and then diligently act upon what you discover. If you do this, you will be like one of the five wise virgins of Matthew chapter 25. You will have enough oil for your lamp so that you are ready to meet the bridegroom when He appears. Of the ten virgins Jesus mentions in this parable, the five who ran out of oil when the bridegroom arrived ended up outside of the wedding ceremony, or basically "out in the cold." This does not have to happen to you.

Now that we have established our objective while examining some key end-time events described in the Bible, let us take a look at how to understand and unpack Scripture. We will consider some necessary ground rules for our study along with fundamental principles that will help us stay focused and on course. Having the appropriate mindset is one thing; laying a solid foundation upon which to build is another. You cannot have one without the other and expect to understand the Bible.

Chapter 2

Choosing the Right Method of Interpretation

Understanding God's Intent

Statisticians are quick to remind us that numbers do not lie. Obvious as this may seem, these same professionals also know that numbers can be manipulated to render a wide variety of desired or skewed outcomes. To avoid this pitfall when interpreting the Bible, **Chapter 1** stressed the importance of reading and studying the Bible on your own rather than developing belief systems based on the opinions of others. **Chapter 2** will take this one step further by discussing the importance of utilizing the most accurate method of biblical interpretation or, in theological terms, the best hermeneutic.

When we approach God's Word to determine its meaning, our desire should be to discover what God is expressing, whether we agree with it or not. If we truly wish to understand Scripture as God meant it to be understood, we must take what we read at **face value**. This is accomplished by seeking the normal, natural, and even cultural sense of the biblical text as the author wrote it to the original audience during the time it was written.

A single verse in Scripture may have several applications but only one true meaning. Failure to accept this principle often results in reading into Scripture biased or personal preferences. A face value hermeneutic helps the reader avoid such tendencies and more accurately guides us down the path of correctly interpreting God's Word.

For our study we will be using English translations of the Bible's original languages. There are many Bible translations, and scholars hold varying opinions as to which ones are most accurate. Those widely accepted as good study Bibles include the New American Standard Bible (NASB), older editions of the New International Version (NIV), both the King James Version and the New King James Version (KJV and NKJV), and the English Standard Version (ESV). (Unless otherwise noted, all quoted passages are taken from the ESV.) In many cases, the translation used would be irrelevant because most of the aforementioned translations accurately portray the intended message. For other passages, one version may be chosen over another for better clarity. Translations that should be avoided when studying Scripture are those that incorporate a more modern prose-like format. Although interesting, and seemingly easier to read, the original intent of the authors can become lost if too much artistic liberty has been taken.

Even relying on English translations derived from the original languages—Greek and Aramaic in the New Testament, and Hebrew in the Old Testament—can have its challenges, as not all words or phrases are easily understood and translated into English. Minute differences can alter intended meaning. There may be times in your ongoing research when you may want to examine a more exact translation, such as Young's Literal Translation, for further clarity on a passage. Though the English structure of such translations can sometimes be challenging to follow, they can help to more accurately capture the author's intended meaning when studying the intricacies of subject and verb agreement, verb tense, placement of phrases within a sentence, etc. This may sound somewhat complicated, but for the most part it is not. You will soon discover that the majority of what we will study is surprisingly easy to understand.

As we approach the principles of face value hermeneutics, there are certain assumptions concerning God and the Bible that must be addressed. Without agreement on these foundational building blocks, unnecessary debate could easily arise that might distract us from the task at hand. If you doubt these assumptions you can certainly read on, but you will probably find yourself with more questions than answers by the time you have finished reading this book.

1. First and foremost, one must believe that the commonly accepted Bible is the actual written Word of God. Though the Holy Spirit inspired human beings to both write and compile the Bible, God is the author (2 Peter 1:21). Through it, God reveals who He is and His plan for the human race. Anything short of accepting this basic premise limits any in-depth biblical study to mere curiosity, relegating the Bible to merely another book.

2. Next, one must believe that God wants His people to have more than a casual understanding of His Word. Though the parables, stories, and descriptions of events revealed in the Bible may challenge our intel-

lect, many of the wonderful mysteries of God become amazingly clear once a face value hermeneutic is used.

3. Because God is omnipotent and without limitations, one must also assume that God is fully capable of making sure we can understand His Word even if, as in our case, we are mainly using English translations of the Bible. Nevertheless, we need to cooperate with Him by doing our best to study His Word wisely, being diligent in our research, and openly seeking His intended meaning of the text and not our own.

4. We cannot proceed in our study without believing that there are no contradictions in Scripture. Apparent contradictions do not imply opposing sides to a given issue. Differences can sometimes arise, but this usually occurs when we do not fully recognize what God intended the original audience to understand about His Word. A thorough search of all related Scriptures on a given subject will eventually reveal the common denominator that makes all the passages come together, bringing to light the correct answer. Such analysis eventually joins all the various pieces of the puzzle in perfect harmony and clarity. Does this mean that a faithful and diligent study of God's Word will always yield total comprehension about every mystery contained in the Bible? By no means. As God told Daniel through the angel Gabriel, there are some things that He will only reveal when He is ready.

   I heard, but I did not understand. Then I said, "O my lord, what shall be the outcome of these things?" He said, "Go your way, Daniel, for the words are shut up and sealed until the time of the end" (Daniel 12:8–9).

5. Finally, when the study of a subject fails to bring the clarity we desire, we should remain attentive and alert to His guidance while awaiting additional insight and understanding.

   "It is like a man going on a journey, when he leaves home and puts his servants in charge, each with his work, and commands the doorkeeper to stay awake. Therefore stay awake—for you do not know when the master of the house will come, in the evening, or at midnight, or when the rooster crows, or in the morning—lest he come suddenly and find you asleep" (Mark 13:34–36).

Admittedly these are not minor assumptions. Nonetheless, proceeding on a pathway toward the serious study of any important biblical topic without these fundamental principles in place leaves us wide open to an array of fragmented conclusions. Believing that God is, that He is more than capable of getting His message out to His people, that He can easily overcome any obstacle hindering clear communication, and that He is without contradiction are all essential for a successful outcome to our study. The daily walk of a true Christ-follower is fueled by faith in these assertions. Lacking this cornerstone of beliefs leaves us vulnerable to being tossed about by every wind of doctrine that may blow our way (Ephesians 4:14).

Five Principles of a Face Value Hermeneutic

With the above foundation in place, let us now move on to examine five fundamental principles of a face value method of interpretation.

It Is Simply A Matter Of When

1. Projecting our own ideas into Scripture is frequently the precursor to misinterpretation. Instead, we are seeking to discover the author's intended meaning at the time any passage was written. Not our will but His be done (Luke 22:42).

2. Just as "location, location, location" is key to success in real estate, "context, context, context" is key to the successful interpretation of biblical text. When studying Scripture, we need to understand the historical setting, whom the author is addressing, and the circumstances surrounding the passage. Also, beware of proof texting. This is taking individual passages, or parts of a passage, out of context to support a man-made idea about what God's Word says. For example, just because Peter and some of the other apostles are quoted as saying, *"We must obey God rather than men"* (Acts 5:29), it does not give us the right to categorically disobey governmental law (Romans 13:1–7).

3. Whenever possible, let Scripture interpret Scripture; let the Bible be your reference guide. The truth behind seemingly difficult passages can frequently be discovered through passages that are more obvious. For example, Jesus told His disciples during the Olivet Discourse to research the book of Daniel for additional understanding concerning His second coming, which we will do in part later. You will find that the book of Daniel adds tremendous clarity to these end-time events.

4. As with other written works, we must determine the real meaning of figures of speech, such as similes and

metaphors, when they are used in the context of passages. Similes, which use the connecting words "like" and "as," and metaphors, that conversely have no connecting words, are common throughout Scripture. Take for example Revelation 12:4b: *"And the dragon stood before the woman who was about to give birth."* At face value this makes little sense. But a few verses later Scripture states, *"And the great dragon was thrown down, that ancient serpent, who is called the devil and Satan, the deceiver of the whole world"* (Revelation 12:9a). In this case, we have a metaphor followed by an instance of Scripture interpreting Scripture.

Writers will often use distinctly expressive words and phrases to characterize people, places, or things. For example, there are numerous descriptors for Jesus throughout the Bible: the Word of God, the Good Shepherd, the Lamb of God, the Son of Man, the Door, the Lion of Judah, the Bread of Life, etc. Another person with multiple descriptors is one called the Antichrist. As your study of end-time events increases, you will discover that he has a major role during the latter days as Satan's ambassador on Earth. Among other things, he is referred to as the beast, the son of destruction, the man of lawlessness, and the prince. Such descriptive language helps reveal exactly who these personalities genuinely are and what is coming.

Idioms, or expressions, are also used in Scripture, such as when the apostle Paul speaks of his *thorn in the flesh*. In another instance, when Paul was on his way to Damascus to persecute Christians, Jesus appeared to him in a vision and said, *"It is hard for you to kick against the goads"* (2 Corinthians 12:7; Acts 26:14). In the first example, Paul did not have a literal thorn piercing his body but apparently some sort of nagging ailment he was praying to be healed of. Likewise, in the second example, Paul (previously called Saul) was not literally kicking against an ox goad, or long pointed stick used to prod livestock pulling carts. Jesus was telling Paul that he was running wildly in the wrong direction in opposition to God's will.

5. Finally, look for both near and far applications of prophetic passages. Many prophecies in the Bible work on these two levels simultaneously. An example of this occurs in chapters 2 and 3 of the book of Revelation. Jesus' instruction, praise, and warnings in His messages to the churches—along with potential judgment and/or reward—are as relevant to the churches scattered throughout the world today as they were to the actual churches in Asia at that time. For a near/far application to be valid, the prophecy in question must allow for this from the face value context and wording of the passage.

The preceding points lay a basic foundation upon which to build and develop our study of end-time events. If we sincerely endeavor to rid our hearts and minds of personal bias, if we believe in God's ability to accurately communicate His message, and if we are ready to accept His written Word at face value as dictated to the original audience, then we should be well equipped to begin our study of the Olivet Discourse.

CHAPTER 3

ON THE ROAD TO THE OLIVET DISCOURSE

THE STONE THE BUILDERS REJECTED (MATTHEW 21:42)

In order to fully appreciate the incredible things Jesus told His disciples on the Mount of Olives, a discourse that occurred just prior to His last meal with them before His betrayal and crucifixion, we need to understand what transpired along the path that brought Him there. Throughout His ministry, Jesus' message remained consistent: believe on Him and be saved or reject Him and face judgment. He offered life, hope, and salvation to all who received Him. His words, actions, and miracles confirmed He was the awaited Messiah. Jesus extended forgiveness and mercy to all that acknowledged their sins. He exposed the hypocrites that claimed they had no guilt and left them to their fate. There was nothing more to say. There would be no excuses left. Let us walk with Jesus along the dusty road that led to the Olivet Discourse when, at the close of His ministry, He tells

His disciples about the supernatural celestial gathering of all those who accept Him and the judgment of the wicked who reject Him.

WATER TURNED TO WINE

During His three-and-a-half-year ministry, Jesus did some amazing things. It all began with His turning water into wine at a wedding banquet.

Think about it.

Jesus' first miracle: turn water into wine—at a wedding banquet.

Jesus did everything for a reason, but this?

Really?

In the story, the master of the feast had basically run out of wine before the festivities were over. So, at His mother Mary's request, Jesus crafted what literally may have been the best wine ever made. He did this using some large water jars—six of them, to be exact—holding anywhere from 20 to 30 gallons each. This is a substantial amount of wine: 120 to 180 gallons, more or less. (In perspective, there were probably a lot of people at that banquet. Remember, there were no movies or TVs back then, much less social media and "smart" cell phones. This would have been the town highlight of the week!)

After Jesus' miracle, there was no further mention of the host running out of wine. The host even commented that he could not believe how good the wine tasted at this point in the wedding feast.

> *When the master of the feast tasted the water now become wine, and did not know where it came from (though the servants who had drawn the water knew), the master of the feast called the bridegroom and said to him, "Everyone serves*

the good wine first, and when people have drunk freely, then the poor wine. But you have kept the good wine until now" (John 2:9–10).

Jesus' first miracle: turn water into wine.

Why?

Let us consider some possibilities.

To prove He could? Not likely. There are many miracles that Jesus, the Creator and Sustainer of of the universe, could have performed to prove His power and authority, yet He chose to do this. He did nothing without a purpose, but why turn water into wine?

To confirm that drinking wine is okay? Though it is common knowledge that Jesus is not against drinking wine, as He did so Himself, this does not appear to be the focus here.

To show He was willing to obey His mother? This is also unlikely. Throughout His ministry, Jesus made it clear that obedience to God is His first priority in spite of what anyone, including family, might say or want.

While he was still speaking to the people, behold, his mother and his brothers stood outside, asking to speak to him. But he replied to the man who told him, "Who is my mother, and who are my brothers?" And stretching out his hand toward his disciples, he said, "Here are my mother and my brothers! For whoever does the will of my Father in heaven is my brother and sister and mother" (Matthew 12:46–50).

So then why? Why turn water into wine at a wedding banquet as your first miracle?

Scripture gives us an indication.

This, the first of his signs, Jesus did at Cana in Galilee, and manifested his glory. And his disciples believed in him (John 2:11).

Because of this miracle, Jesus' disciples believed. It must have certainly caught their attention.

But again, why turn water into wine to make them take notice?

During His ministry Jesus compared His works, sayings, and teachings to *new wine*. He also indicated who would readily receive them.

"No one sews a patch of unshrunk cloth on an old garment, for the patch will pull away from the garment, making the tear worse. Neither do people pour new wine into old wineskins. If they do, the skins will burst; the wine will run out and the wineskins will be ruined. No, they pour new wine into new wineskins, and both are preserved" (Matthew 9:16–17 NIV).

Jesus said that only *new wineskins* would be able to hold what He has to say. This miracle might be a metaphor indicating that only those who are new in spirit, and open to His teaching, will be filled with His *new wine*.

But why choose a wedding banquet?

News probably spread quickly about the huge jars of "water turned into wine" miracle. This wedding banquet, likely the biggest social event in town, would seem a perfect venue to spread the message that someone very special is making an impact in Israel, someone they should probably watch very closely.

Water turned into wine at a wedding. Jesus' first miracle is only a foreshadowing of something far greater to come.

Then I heard what seemed to be the voice of a great multitude, like the roar of many waters and like the sound of mighty peals of thunder, crying out,

"Hallelujah! For the Lord our God the Almighty reigns. Let us rejoice and exult and give him the glory, for the marriage of the Lamb has come, and his Bride has made herself ready; it was granted her to clothe herself with fine linen, bright and pure"—for the fine linen is the righteous deeds of the saints.

And the angel said to me, "Write this: Blessed are those who are invited to the marriage supper of the Lamb." And he said to me, "These are the true words of God." Then I fell down at his feet to worship him, but he said to me, "You must not do that! I am a fellow servant with you and your brothers who hold to the testimony of Jesus. Worship God." For the testimony of Jesus is the spirit of prophecy (Revelation 19:6–10).

The road to the Mount of Olives is just beginning.

As His ministry continued, Jesus healed the sick, gave sight to the blind, multiplied food to feed the crowds, and even raised the dead. But though He performed many incredible miracles, and spent countless hours teaching about godly living and the wonders of the kingdom of God, Jesus also made one thing clear throughout His entire ministry: judgment is coming to all who refuse to believe on Him.

Let us take a closer look.

John the Baptist, Jesus' cousin and the one God chose to prepare the way for Jesus' ministry, made this scathing statement to the religious leaders who came to see—and question—why he was baptizing:

"You brood of vipers! Who warned you to flee from the wrath to come? Bear fruit in keeping with repentance. And do not presume to say to yourselves, 'We have Abraham as our father,' for I tell you, God is able from these stones to raise up children for Abraham. Even now the axe is laid to the root of the trees. Every tree therefore that does not bear good fruit is cut down and thrown into the fire. I baptize you with water for repentance, but he who is coming after me is mightier than I, whose sandals I am not worthy to carry. He will baptize you with the Holy Spirit and fire. His winnowing fork is in his hand, and he will clear his threshing floor and gather his wheat into the barn, but the chaff he will burn with unquenchable fire" (Matthew 3:7–12).

With the stage fully set by John for Jesus' ministry, Jesus gives His own words of warning to what He called a foolish, faithless, and perverse generation. In the parable of the wise and foolish builders Jesus said:

"And everyone who hears these words of mine and does not do them will be like a foolish man who built his house on the sand. And the rain fell, and the floods came, and the winds blew and beat against that house, and it fell, and great was the fall of it" (Matthew 7:26–27).

There is more, so much more.

On one occasion, Jesus healed the servant of a Roman centurion because of the centurion's great faith. This Roman commander, who clearly was a God-fearing man, was obviously not an Israelite. Subsequently, Jesus said to those of His own people that had no faith in Him:

"I tell you, many will come from east and west and recline at table with Abraham, Isaac, and Jacob in the kingdom of heaven, while the sons of the kingdom will be thrown into the outer darkness. In that place there will be weeping and gnashing of teeth" (Matthew 8:11–12).

Jesus makes it known that admission into the kingdom of heaven would be coming to non-Jewish peoples all over the world. Being from the natural line of Abraham would guarantee nothing.

Before sending His disciples out to preach in the towns of Galilee, He told them:

"And if anyone will not receive you or listen to your words, shake off the dust from your feet when you leave that house or town. Truly, I say to you, it will be more bearable on the day of judgment for the land of Sodom and Gomorrah than for that town" (Matthew 10:14–15).

If you want to see these verses in perspective, read Genesis chapters 18 and 19 in the Old Testament about the destruction of Sodom and Gomorrah. Jesus refers to this sobering event more than once.

After warning His disciples of the persecution they would face because they follow Him and spread His teachings, Jesus declares:

"So everyone who acknowledges me before men, I also will acknowledge before my Father who is in heaven, but whoever denies me before men, I also will deny before my Father who is in heaven" (Matthew 10:32–33).

In Matthew chapter 11, Jesus begins denouncing *"the cities where most of his mighty works had been done, because they did not repent"* (verse 20). Ending with the city of Capernaum, Jesus declares in verse 24:

"But I tell you that it will be more tolerable on the day of judgment for the land of Sodom than for you."

With multitudes of people following Jesus, the religious leadership became increasingly uneasy about Him. They were constantly looking for ways to trip Him up and accuse Him of being anything but a man of God, much less the Son of God. Along with some of the crowds, they said that Jesus:

- Was a blasphemer: Matthew 9:3, Mark 2:7, John 10:33
- Drove out demons by Beelzebub, the prince of demons: Matthew 9:34, 12:24; Mark 3:22; Luke 11:15
- Was demon possessed: Mark 3:22; John 7:20, 8:48, 10:20
- Was a glutton and drunkard, a friend of tax collectors and sinners: Matthew 11:19
- Was a sinner: John 9:24
- Was raving mad and out of His mind: Mark 3:21, John 10:20
- Was a Samaritan or, as far as they were concerned, a half-breed and not a full-blooded son of Abraham: John 8:48

(Note: The animosity between the Samaritans and the Jews dates back to the book of Genesis when Joseph, the favorite son of Jacob [Israel], was despised by his brothers who plotted to get rid of him [Genesis 37:3–4]. This former bitterness resurfaced when the nation of Israel was divided in two. The northern kingdom, which eventually became known as Samaria and was partially comprised of the descendants of Joseph, intermarried with their foreign invaders and began worshiping their pagan idols along with the Lord their God [2 Kings 17:24–41]. This infuriated their "pure-blooded" brethren from the south. As a result, the hatred between them grew and continued for centuries.)

For those religious leaders that believed they were accurately following the Law of Moses, the thing that irritated them the most was what Jesus and His disciples did on the Sabbath day.

- His disciples picked grain in the fields to eat on the Sabbath because they were hungry: Matthew 12:1–2, Luke 6:2.
- Jesus frequently healed people on the Sabbath. This so angered the religious leaders that they wanted to kill Him: Matthew 12:10–14, Mark 3:1–6, Luke 6:6–11, John 5:18.
- They concluded that Jesus was not from God because—according to them—He did not keep the Sabbath: John 9:16.

Up to this point the religious establishment might have already come to their conclusions about Jesus and His teachings, but Jesus had also come to His own conclusion about them. As recounted in Matthew chapter 23, when Jesus walked the temple grounds in Jerusalem one last time as a free man, He held nothing back. Addressing the crowds in the temple, Jesus offers His analysis of Israel's religious leaders:

"The scribes and the Pharisees sit on Moses' seat, so do and observe whatever they tell you, but not the works they do. For they preach, but do not practice. They tie up heavy burdens, hard to bear, and lay them on people's shoulders, but they themselves are not willing to move them with their finger" (Matthew 23:2–4).

Shortly after this, Jesus turns to address the religious leaders directly and calls them hypocrites, blind guides and fools, whitewashed tombs full of dead men's bones and everything unclean, as well as snakes and vipers. He is fed up with their lack of faith, their inability to perceive the truth and purpose behind the law, and their constant rejection of Him and His Word. He knew of their plot to arrest Him, that they paid Judas to betray Him, that they would make false accusations to incriminate Him, that they would sway the crowds against Him, and that they would convince the Romans to crucify Him. Before leaving the temple, Jesus concludes with this:

"O Jerusalem, Jerusalem, the city that kills the prophets and stones those who are sent to it! How often would I have gathered your children together as a hen gathers her brood under her wings, and you were not willing! See, your house is left to you desolate. For I tell you, you will not see me again, until you say, 'Blessed is he who comes in the name of the Lord'" (Matthew 23:37–39).

Jesus' open ministry to those other than His disciples is now over. He has declared His judgment on the ones that have blatantly rejected Him. For three and a half years it has all been building up to this very moment. He knows what is about to happen. His emotions are undoubtedly running high as He leaves the temple grounds. Yet it soon becomes obvious that His disciples still had virtually no clue what was really happening. At least some of them had their eyes fixed on the beauty and majesty of the temple buildings. Jesus, on the other hand, was focused on His coming crucifixion, His subsequent resurrection, the fulfillment of God's promises of redemption for those that believe, and the end of the world as we know it.

And so His discourse begins.

Chapter 4

The Olivet Discourse, Part 1
(Matthew 24:1–14)

Not as Complicated as You Might Think

A Few Facts
The first four books of the New Testament—written by Matthew, Mark, Luke, and John—are known as the Gospels. The Olivet Discourse is referenced in the first three. The most detailed account appears in chapters 24 and 25 of Matthew. The books of Mark and Luke cover this discourse to a lesser degree, but they offer some additional insight (Mark 13, Luke 21:5–36). The book of John is the only Gospel where it is not mentioned.

The Olivet Discourse is Jesus' own account of the events surrounding His second coming. Although Jesus does not offer an actual timeline of specific dates in His discourse, He does outline a distinct order of events. He also describes some important signs to watch for, signs indicating that His return to Earth, and the end of things as we know them, is close at hand.

Jesus understands what it takes to build a strong and durable building:

"Everyone who comes to me and hears my words and does them, I will show you what he is like: he is like a man building a house, who dug deep and laid the foundation on the rock. And when a flood arose, the stream broke against that house and could not shake it, because it had been well built" (Luke 6:47–48).

Knowing this, Jesus speaks very specifically to His disciples about the events surrounding His return. In the Olivet Discourse He leaves no doubt as to what will come to pass, and in what order. As you will see, Jesus lays an amazingly solid foundation.

Satan, the distorter and twister of truth, also knows the immense importance of this discourse and has been working relentlessly over the past two millennia to taint its message, cast doubt on its simplicity, and confuse God's people. Hence, the controversy over Jesus' second coming begins right here with the Olivet Discourse.

Before going any further, take a moment and read Matthew chapters 24 and 25 on your own. Follow all the principles we have already established in the previous chapters. Clear your mind and set aside any preconceived ideas. Just read the text. Imagine you are there—right there—with Jesus on the Mount of Olives. The Son of God is speaking. What are you hearing? What do you see?

At first glance it should seem fairly cut and dried, or at least a good part of it. Jesus has just left the temple in Jerusalem after blasting its leadership for their hardness of heart, unbelief, and hypocrisy (Matthew chapter 23). He has little left to say to them. Except for maybe a few, they have already made up their minds. Their fate is sealed and their judgment is imminent.

As Jesus leaves the temple grounds with His disciples, He is quite possibly reflecting on the short time He has left on Earth and some very important things remaining to tell them. He is also keenly aware of the suffering He is about to face. Then, out of virtually nowhere and quite likely oblivious to the battle being waged within their rabbi, one of the disciples approaches Jesus. Perhaps trying to lighten the moment after Jesus' confrontation with the unbelieving spiritual leaders of His people, the disciple points to the temple buildings and their apparent magnificence.

What is Jesus' response?

"Do you see these great buildings? There will not be left here one stone upon another that will not be thrown down" (Mark 13:2).

The disciples' minds were still very much attuned to the physical and the present. They could not discern the incredible events that were soon to transpire, events that would forever reshape their understanding of God's plan for the human race. Jesus was fixed on the impending judgment of God, the redemption of the few, the wondrous future of His kingdom, and the extremely painful sacrifice He would soon endure to bring it all to fruition.

Some of the other disciples were within earshot of the conversation. It is easy to imagine their astonishment at Jesus' words. Certainly for such a disastrous thing to happen to their sacred and holy temple it would take a major earth-shattering event!

After redressing the religious establishment, Jesus left Jerusalem and sat on the Mount of Olives just outside of Jerusalem. Peter, James, John, and Andrew could wait no longer. They had to know what Jesus was talking about. Approaching Him privately (Mark 13:3), they asked Him two important questions (Matthew 24:3 KJV).

1. When will these things happen?
2. What will be the sign of Your coming and the end of the world?

It is obvious from the disciples' line of questioning what they are assuming. Certainly, the only way their temple and its grounds could possibly come to ruin would be at the end of the world. Since Jesus knows this is not the case, He lovingly and methodically answers both questions with such clarity as to leave no doubt what will happen and what should be done.

Let us examine Jesus' discourse, as recounted in Matthew, verse by verse.

"See that no one leads you astray. For many will come in my name, saying, 'I am the Christ,' and they will lead many astray" (verses 4–5).

At first glance, this seems to be about individuals falsely claiming to be the Messiah. Even during Old Testament times the Lord warned His people about false prophets. (See Jeremiah 5:31 and 14:14.) Many infamous names can be listed in this category. But there is another possibility, one that initially might not be so obvious: groups and organizations, as well-meaning and well-intentioned as they may appear, claiming to be Christ's true church yet teaching theology contrary to Scripture. There are many that are deceiving and being deceived in the name of Christ.

"And you will hear of wars and rumors of wars. See that you are not alarmed, for this must take place, but the end is not yet. For nation will rise against nation, and kingdom against kingdom" (verses 6–7a).

Our planet has experienced countless wars, and wars continue to be waged. But we, as Christ-followers, are not to be alarmed for *the end is not yet.*

"... and there will be famines and earthquakes in various places" (verse 7b).

Reports of famines and earthquakes abound, with ever-increasing frequency.

"All these are but the beginning of the birth pains" (verse 8).

This is an important metaphor, one that Jesus is using to help us understand what will begin to occur before His second coming.

For a mother's birth canal to be fully prepared for the natural delivery of her child, her womb must pass through a series of preparatory stages that thin the wall of her uterus. This process begins with contractions that are generally intermittent and light. In time they become substantially more frequent and intense. As Jesus' return draws closer, we will see all these signs—earthquakes, famines, wars, and the deceptive practices of those claiming to be Christ—growing in frequency and intensity. Historical records of natural disasters will regularly be surpassed as the end approaches.

"Then they will deliver you up to tribulation and put you to death, and you will be hated by all nations for my name's sake. And then many will fall away and betray one another and hate one another. And many false prophets will arise and lead many astray" (verses 9–11).

Many governments of the world are pushing vigorously to enact laws contrary to God's plan for humanity while claiming they are simply safeguarding individual freedoms and personal rights. Books like the Bible will likely be seen as narrow-minded—or even closed-minded—and full of bigotry. Those adhering to the Bible's literal teachings will be labeled dangerous to modern society. The only churches that will openly survive are those that succumb to the pressures of secular ideologies. All others will be maligned and either persecuted or driven into hiding. Many professing

Christians have been deceived by such modernist thinking and will increasingly align themselves with these movements. Some will even betray the true church while actually believing they are pleasing God (John 16:2).

"And because lawlessness will be increased, the love of many will grow cold. But the one who endures to the end will be saved" (verses 12–13).

Holding fast to God's Word, and living a life of love and sacrifice no matter how challenging or gloomy the surrounding circumstances, is paramount.

"And this gospel of the kingdom will be proclaimed throughout the whole world as a testimony to all nations, and then the end will come" (verse 14).

It is important to remember that the *gospel of the kingdom* is not just the good news of salvation by grace but the totality of Jesus' message contained in the first four books of the New Testament. It includes this very message Jesus is delivering to His disciples on the Mount of Olives about His return. Bible translation is rapidly increasing. In only a short matter of time *the whole world* will have the opportunity to hear the entire gospel.

Yet there is one more possibility when the *eternal gospel* will be proclaimed to all who *dwell on earth*.

Then I saw another angel flying directly overhead, with an eternal gospel to proclaim to those who dwell on earth, to every nation and tribe and language and people. And he said with a loud voice, "Fear God and give him glory, because the hour of his judgment has come, and worship him who made heaven and earth, the sea and the springs of water" (Revelation 14:6–7).

Though we have much to cover in our end-time study before we consider the book of Revelation, I think it is important to mention that what is recounted in this passage—according to a face value hermeneutic—is absolutely real and only one of the many wonderful and amazing things that will happen during the latter days. According to what is written above, the whole world will definitely hear about God's judgment right before the end. Look closely at the context of these verses and then you decide.

As we move into the next part of the Olivet Discourse contained in Matthew 24:15–31, Jesus outlines some pivotal events and the order in which they will occur. Any reasonable analysis or discussion of the end times cannot exclude this series of verses. Their impact is immense. As self-explanatory as they may appear, their words bring some people great joy while raising questions for others whose doctrinal beliefs are contrary to what the text actually states. Those in the latter category tend to use complex reasoning to try and explain that what Jesus says is not actually what He means.

One of the primary controversies is this: To whom is Jesus actually speaking here? Some argue that the book of Matthew was written specifically for the Jews of His time. They say this discourse is a serious warning about events that would soon take place either within or near their time. True to this reasoning, in AD 70 Titus and his Roman army invaded Jerusalem, wreaked havoc on the Jewish people, and destroyed the temple so that not one stone was left upon another, just as Jesus foretold. Because of this, some further suggest that everything stated in the Olivet Discourse has already taken place. But if this were the case, Jesus would have already returned and everyone on Earth would have seen Him—literally and not figuratively—as outlined in verses 27 through 30. It takes a lot of work to explain such statements away. When you add the fact that the Olivet Discourse is also covered in the books of Mark and Luke, books that are not considered to be written specifically for the Jews, I would suggest that Jesus' words in this discourse reach far beyond the events of AD 70 and will impact many people yet to come, Jew and non-Jew alike.

Too many scholars have spent vast amounts of time endeavoring to "correct" the overwhelming simplicity of Jesus' own account of His coming and the accompanying events. Why? Divide and conquer, confuse and scatter. As mentioned earlier, this is one of Satan's primary tactics. It is just another reminder that this is not about our will or what we want but about God's truth and His plan for humanity. He wants us to understand—and we can understand if we remain focused and stay true to the simple reading of His Word.

Let us now consider some of the central verses in Jesus' message.

CHAPTER 5

THE OLIVET DISCOURSE, PART 2
(MATTHEW 24:15–31)

NOT AS EASY AS WE WOULD LIKE

In **Chapter 2** we looked at five basic principles of a face value hermeneutic, or method of interpretation. One of them, the near/far implication and application of some prophetic Scriptures, comes to life in Matthew 24:15–31. In the near sense, some of these verses contained important instructions for Jesus' disciples when Titus invaded Jerusalem in AD 70. In the long term, there is even greater application for His disciples who will be alive at the time of His return. Either way, Jesus' message is the same to all: watch for the signs and be prepared.

"*So when you see the **abomination of desolation** spoken of by the prophet Daniel, standing in the holy place (let the reader understand)*" (verse 15, emphasis added).

What we should consider in verse 15:

1) The use of *when*.
2) The *holy place*.
3) Jesus' *let the reader understand* reference to Daniel concerning the **abomination of desolation**.

Let us examine each of the above.

1) You will begin to see a distinct pattern of words used to outline a specific order of events such as *when, then, immediately after,* and *at that time.* It is evident from the text that there is no jumping around. The events outlined are sufficiently described to leave no doubt as to what will happen and in what order. This is where faith in God's Word, just as it is written, is vital. Those who are alive during these times will certainly want to understand and be prepared. As you will soon discover, they will also witness some fascinating and supernatural events.

2) The temple in Jerusalem is generally considered to be the holy place. Some scholars believe there is a specific location within the temple where this abomination will be placed. For additional information we turn to 2 Thessalonians 2:1–4. The apostle Paul writes,

> *Now concerning the coming of our Lord Jesus Christ and our being gathered together to him, we ask you, brothers, not to be quickly shaken in mind or alarmed, either by a spirit or a spoken word, or a letter seeming to be from us, to the effect that the day of the Lord has come. Let no one deceive you in any way. For that day will not come, unless the rebellion* [or *"apostasy"* (NASB), which some believe to be the great falling away from God as per Matthew 24:10–11] *comes first, and the man of lawlessness* [final antichrist] *is revealed, the son of destruction, who opposes and exalts himself against every so-called god or object of worship, so that he takes his seat in the temple of God, proclaiming himself to be God.*

Either way—whether it is the temple in general or a specific location inside—it is apparent that an **abomination of desolation**, placed by *the man of lawlessness*, will somehow be *standing* in the temple during the time of the end prior to the Lord's return.

3) Jesus' reference to the book of Daniel, followed by *let the reader understand* in verse 15, is not a casual comment. Jesus is making the writings of Daniel required reading in order to fully comprehend what He is teaching. As mentioned earlier in **Chapter 1**, there are numerous instances where Jesus is quoted as saying, *"He who has ears to hear, let him hear."* However, it is only during the Olivet Discourse when He is noted in Scripture as emphasizing the research of a specific Old Testament text for additional information.

An **abomination that causes desolation** is mentioned in chapters 9 and 11 of the book of Daniel. The fact that Jesus is referencing Daniel in relation to this event automatically places something within these passages that will coincide with His second coming. In addition to Titus' invasion in AD 70, there have been other occasions in Israel's history when the temple in Jerusalem was defiled by an antichrist figure. One of the most vivid examples was during the reign of Antiochus IV Epiphanes (175–164 BC), who savagely persecuted the Jews in Jerusalem and profaned their temple. But the abomination Jesus is speaking of in His discourse is set up directly preceding His second coming by a final antichrist claiming to be God and initiating the worst period of *tribulation* the world has ever seen. According to the context, this has not yet happened.

Continuing on with Matthew 24:

"*... then let those who are in Judea flee to the mountains. Let the one who is on the housetop not go down to take what is in his house, and let the one who is in the field not turn back to take his cloak*" (verses 16–18).

Jesus' explicit instruction to *those who are in Judea*: when you see the temple being overrun and desecrated, it is time to get out of town, and fast. Retrieve nothing. Head to the high country and do not look back. Lot's wife looked back when Sodom and Gomorrah were being destroyed, and she became a pillar of salt (Genesis chapter 19). Those who were alive in AD 70 and heeded Jesus' warning when Titus laid siege to Jerusalem had the opportunity to survive the onslaught. The overwhelming majority of those that did not, but instead remained in Jerusalem, suffered horrendously at the hands of the Romans. Were these instructions just meant for the Jews in Jerusalem during Titus' invasion? Or is it also prophetic advice for all believers that are alive when Jesus returns?

Concerning the same event, Luke recounts this from Jesus' Olivet Discourse:

"*Likewise, just as it was in the days of Lot—they were eating and drinking, buying and selling, planting and building, but on the day when Lot went out from Sodom, fire and sulfur rained from heaven and destroyed them all—so will it be on the day when the Son of Man is revealed. On that day, let the one who is on the housetop, with his goods in the house, not come down to take them away, and likewise let the one who is in the field not turn back. Remember Lot's wife*" (Luke 17:28–32).

Such intentional repetition of explicit warning should help create a lasting memory for all of Jesus' followers that are alive when He returns.

Back to Matthew 24:

"And alas for women who are pregnant and for those who are nursing infants in those days! Pray that your flight may not be in winter, or on a Sabbath" (verses 19–20).

It would be challenging to run while pregnant, nursing young children, or during the cold of winter. Aside from this, Jewish tradition restricted a Sabbath day's journey to a distance just over half a mile. Rushing toward the hills on the Sabbath would have certainly drawn unwanted attention. But take a closer look. Jesus is making another powerful statement here.

He is telling us to pray.

The overall framework of the end times may be set, but we do not have to idly sit back and do nothing while unprecedented turmoil pummels Earth. Jesus is saying we have the ability to influence some details within the events He is describing. We can actually make a difference, a significant difference. Jesus' admonition is not just to watch. We are to watch and pray. These times will be troublesome enough already. Though prayer is another major biblical topic, and one of the most neglected privileges God has given His children, suffice it to say for our study that we can most definitely make these strenuous times easier if we pray.

*"For then there will be **great tribulation**, such as has not been from the beginning of the world until now, no, and never will be"* (verse 21, emphasis added).

As tragic and brutal as history portrays Titus' invasion of Jerusalem in AD 70, there have been greater horrors unleashed by humanity since then. World War II, with the atomic bomb and the Holocaust, is but one example. Estimates place the total casualties of WWII somewhere between 50 and 80 million people. Atrocities have far from ceased. They have only increased in devastation, scope, and magnitude, just like the birth pangs Jesus alluded to. This final *tribulation*, directly preceding Jesus' second coming, will be the worst the world has ever seen. Nothing that has already happened on Earth will compare to it, and nothing like it will ever happen again. It is hard to put this into perspective.

"And if those days had not been cut short, no human being would be saved. But for the sake of the elect those days will be cut short" (verse 22).

Though other passages of Scripture shed additional light on this, particularly in the books of Daniel and Revelation, we can surmise at this point that the **great tribulation** will somehow be shortened for the sake of His elect.

"Then [or *At that time, NIV*] *if anyone says to you, 'Look, here is the Christ,' or 'There he is!' do not believe it. For false christs and false prophets will arise and perform great signs and wonders, so as to lead astray, if possible, even the elect. See, I have told you beforehand. So if they say to you, 'Look, he is in the wilderness,' do not go out. If they say, 'Look, he is in the inner rooms,' do not believe it. For as the lightning comes from the east and shines as far as the west, so will be the coming of the Son of Man. Wherever the corpse is, there the vultures will gather"* (verses 23–28).

The last sentence, verse 28, requires a closer look. Here in Matthew the English word *corpse* is translated from the Greek word *ptōma*, which means lifeless or dead body. In a similar verse found in Luke 17:37—which we will examine in **Chapter 6**—Luke uses a different Greek word for body, *sōmah*, which refers to a wholly sound or alive body. Though Matthew 24:28 and Luke 17:37 are both recounted from Jesus' Olivet Discourse, their specific contexts within the discourse, and respective meanings, are very different.

Let us look at the context of Matthew 24:28. Is this verse about Jesus' gathering of the elect, as is frequently suggested, or something else?

In Matthew, the English word *vultures* in the ESV Bible is translated from the Greek word *aetós*. It has frequently been translated as eagles but can also refer to other large-winged birds of prey. Older Bible translations stick with eagles, but newer translations use the word *vultures,* as eagles seldom feed off of carrion or the decaying dead. With Matthew choosing the Greek word for a dead body, the utilization of the English word *vultures* in the ESV instead of eagles seems considerably more appropriate.

Jesus once told the Sadducees, a Jewish religious order that did not believe in the resurrection, *"[God] is not God of the dead, but of the living"* (Matthew 22:32, Mark 12:27, Luke 20:38). So rather than Matthew 24:28 being about a gathering to a living Jesus, it would seem more fitting that Jesus is declaring the *false christs and false prophets* as virtually dead while calling those following them *vultures*. Jesus said to some wanting to follow Him, *"Follow me, and leave the dead to bury their own dead"* (Matthew 8:22). For those who reject Jesus and His Word, their fate is set.

Jesus' *lightning* analogy in this passage is also a clear illustration of just how obvious His arrival will be. We are not to listen to anyone saying they have found Him alive on Earth, even if accompanied by *great signs and wonders*. If we know God's Word, we should not be deceived. Jesus' reappearance on Earth from the heavenly realms will be quite a spectacle and evident to all.

So, is Matthew 24:28 about Jesus and His gathering of the elect or about the false christs and false prophets and their dead followers? You decide.

"Immediately after the tribulation of those days the sun will be darkened, and the moon will not give its light, and the stars will fall from heaven, and the powers of the heavens will be shaken. Then will appear in heaven the sign of the

It is Simply A Matter Of When

Son of Man, and then all the tribes of the earth will mourn, and they will see the Son of Man coming on the clouds of heaven with power and great glory" (verses 29–30).

In the Old Testament, Joel makes reference to this same event during the time of God's judgment:

Multitudes, multitudes, in the valley of decision! For the day of the Lord is near in the valley of decision. The sun and the moon are darkened, and the stars withdraw their shining. The Lord roars from Zion, and utters his voice from Jerusalem, and the heavens and the earth quake. But the Lord is a refuge to his people, a stronghold to the people of Israel (Joel 3:14–16).

There are differences, depending on context, as to exactly who God's people are throughout Scripture. Sometimes the text clearly indicates it is about the physical descendants of Israel, or the Jews. Other times *his people* include both the Jews and Gentiles that have accepted Jesus as the Messiah. Unless clearly designated in the text, it all depends on the context. For our study, you can safely assume it is speaking about all of God's children, Jew and Gentile alike, who profess Jesus as the Christ unless otherwise stated.

Back to Matthew:

"[*Immediately after the tribulation of those days* (verse 29)] ... *he will send out his angels with a loud trumpet call, and they will gather his elect from the four winds, from one end of heaven to the other"* (verse 31).

Though Jesus may have been partially referring to Titus' invasion of Jerusalem when addressing His disciples, He was also referring to something far beyond. How do we know this? Jesus' second coming, as described here and in other passages, obviously did not take place *immediately after* the invasion of Jerusalem by Titus. Scripture tells us that when

Jesus returns, His reappearance will be visible to everyone. Aside from verses 29 and 30 in Matthew 24, John says the following in the book of Revelation:

Behold, he is coming with the clouds, and every eye will see him, even those who pierced him, and all tribes of the earth will wail on account of him. Even so. Amen (Revelation 1:7).

The *elect* are God's chosen people. How they are chosen is not a topic for this study. But ultimately, only God knows who His elect are. As followers of Jesus, the best indication we have that a person is one of God's chosen is by his or her *fruit*. Such fruit may not be made manifest until the latter part of someone's life—years after many mistakes, disgraces, and/or failures. For this reason, God's Word states that we should defend His truth but not judge others. Jesus said,

"Beware of false prophets, who come to you in sheep's clothing but inwardly are ravenous wolves. You will recognize them by their fruits. Are grapes gathered from thornbushes, or figs from thistles? So, every healthy tree bears good fruit, but the diseased tree bears bad fruit. A healthy tree cannot bear bad fruit, nor can a diseased tree bear good fruit. Every tree that does not bear good fruit is cut down and thrown into the fire. Thus you will recognize them by their fruits" (Matthew 7:15–20).

"Be merciful, even as your Father is merciful. Judge not, and you will not be judged; condemn not, and you will not be condemned; forgive, and you will be forgiven" (Luke 6:36–37).

Concerning the gathering of the *elect* mentioned in verse 31, a minimal amount of background is needed. In AD 382/383, Pope Damasus commissioned Jerome, a young scholar, to translate the Greek manuscripts of the New Testament and the Greek translation of the Old Testament into Latin. (Some believe Jerome translated the

Old Testament directly from the Hebrew text.) This translation became known as the Vulgate, meaning "common" or "current." Much of modern-day English theological terminology was derived from this Latin translation. Two such terms relating to the end times are "rapture" and "advent."

Rapture was derived from the Latin word *rapere*, meaning to seize, which itself was translated from the Greek verb *harpazo*, meaning to catch away. Advent is derived from the Latin word *adventus*, meaning arrival, translated from the Greek word *parousia*. Both are key words to describe Jesus' coming. They served their purpose in Latin translations but are not specific enough for English. They are found nowhere in our English translations, yet they have tended to create a considerable amount of confusion among Bible scholars regarding the exact timing of Jesus' second coming. Some believe the rapture (gathering) and advent (Jesus' return) are two separate events. If we look closely at Jesus' discourse, I believe we will find the answer.

In verses 30 and 31 of Matthew 24, we see the Son of Man—Jesus—coming on the clouds and sending His angels to gather His elect *from the four winds, from one end of the heavens to the other*. The fact that this states His angels are gathering His elect from the heavens is proof, to some, that the rapture has already taken place and that He is only gathering His elect that are already there. For this reason it is so important to research all related verses in order to obtain the entire picture. We find additional information on this gathering in Mark's account of the Olivet Discourse:

> *"And then they will see the Son of Man coming in clouds with great power and glory. And then he will send out the angels and gather his elect from the four winds, from the ends of the earth to the ends of heaven"* (Mark 13:26–27).

When writing to the Thessalonians, the apostle Paul brings even further clarity.

For this we declare to you by a word from the Lord, that we who are alive, who are left until the coming of the Lord, will not precede those who have fallen asleep. For the Lord himself will descend from heaven with a cry of command, with the voice of an archangel, and with the sound of the trumpet of God. And the dead in Christ will rise first. Then we who are alive, who are left, will be caught up together with them in the clouds to meet the Lord in the air, and so we will always be with the Lord (1 Thessalonians 4:15–17).

Paul's words blend perfectly with the Olivet Discourse. From verses 30 and 31 in Matthew 24, along with these verses in Mark 13 and 1 Thessalonians 4, we see that Jesus returns from the heavenly realms with a grand announcement. He sends His angels to gather His elect from heaven and Earth, both living and dead, and they will be with Him forever. When does all this happen? It happens *immediately after* the unparalleled *tribulation* that engulfs Earth, when the sun and moon are darkened, the stars fall from the sky, and the heavenly bodies are shaken. Are you seeing an unmistakable order here?

Let us outline the complete sequence of events described in the Olivet Discourse through verse 31 of Matthew chapter 24 along with the other supporting verses mentioned above.

Concerning the temple, Jesus told His disciples:

- The temple in Jerusalem will be completely destroyed.
- Not one stone of the temple will be left on top of another.

It is Simply A Matter Of When

Questions that Jesus' disciples asked Him:

- When will the temple be destroyed?
- *What will be the sign of your coming and the sign of the close of the age?*

Jesus describes what He calls the beginning of birth pangs:

- *Many will come* in His name, falsely deceiving many.
- There will be *wars and rumors of wars*, but we are not to be alarmed, as the end is still to come.
- *Nation will rise against nation, and kingdom against kingdom.*
- *There will be famines and earthquakes in various places.*

Next:

- You will be handed over to be persecuted and put *to death*.
- *You will be hated by all nations* because of your belief in Jesus.
- Many will turn away from the faith and will *betray one another and hate one another.*
- *Many false prophets will arise and lead many astray.*
- *And because lawlessness will be increased, the love of many will grow cold.*
- *But the one who endures to the end will be saved.*
- *And this gospel of the kingdom will be proclaimed throughout the whole world as a testimony to all nations, and then the end will come.*

When the ***abomination of desolation*** stands *in the holy place*, as described by Daniel the prophet:

- *Then let those who are in Judea flee to the mountains.*
- Do not go back from the field, or into your house, to gather anything.
- It will be hard for pregnant and nursing mothers.
- *Pray that your flight may not be in the winter or on a Sabbath.*

For then:

- There will be unparalleled *tribulation* on Earth.
- *For the sake of the elect, these days* [of *tribulation*] *will be cut short* or no one would survive.
- Do not believe anyone who says they know where the Christ is.
- Those declaring themselves to be the Christ or a prophet will perform great signs and miracles, attempting to deceive even the elect—*if possible.*
- *For as the lightning comes from the east and shines as far as the west, so will be the coming of the Son of Man.*
- *Where the corpse is, there the vultures will gather.*

Immediately after the *tribulation*:

- *The sun will be darkened.*
- *The moon will not give its light.*
- *The stars will fall from heaven.*
- *The powers of the heavens will be shaken.*

Then:

- *Will appear in heaven the sign of the Son of Man.*
- *All the tribes of the earth will mourn.*

- *They will see the Son of Man coming on the clouds of heaven with power and great glory.*
- *He will send out His angels with a loud trumpet call* to gather His elect from the far corners of the heavens and Earth.

The narrative is straightforward. History shows that Titus and his army invaded Jerusalem and completely destroyed the temple. Jesus told His disciples to leave Jerusalem, head for the hills, and not look back as soon as they realize it is happening. Does this also apply to us? Was the Olivet Discourse fulfilled with the invasion of Titus and his army in AD 70? I believe you will find the answer is indisputable. Jesus' return, as described in His own words, has not yet happened. Those who insinuate that His return has already happened, either symbolically or spiritually, are misreading the text and potentially leading others astray.

As we build our sequence of events and timeline piece by piece, we will discover:

- Those things we consider to be fact.
- Those things that appear obvious, though are not necessarily fact.
- Those things we can only speculate as to what they are.
- Those things we do not yet know.

There is nothing wrong with speculation. The Lord wants us to keep our eyes and ears open, watching for the signs of His coming—as best we can—based on what we currently understand. What we should avoid is declaring speculation to be fact. By doing so, we tend to harden our hearts and minds against seeing things differently as the signs of His coming become more obvious. In light of the above, let us take a closer look at what we should recognize so far:

- Titus invaded Jerusalem, destroyed the temple, and wreaked havoc on the Jews in AD 70: Fact.
- The Jews that endured *to the end* and heeded Jesus' warning—without being dissuaded otherwise by false prophets—and immediately fled the invasion of Jerusalem by Titus were saved: Highly likely.
- Jesus' return, as described in His own words, did not occur *immediately after* Titus' invasion and the destruction of the temple. Therefore the **great tribulation**—along with the sign in the sun, moon and stars, the coming of the Son of Man, and the rapture or gathering of His elect from the heavens and Earth—is yet to come: According to Jesus' description of events, this is fact.
- Titus' invasion was an obvious near fulfillment of Jesus' prophecy. Since Jesus did not return immediately afterwards, the far fulfillment will follow the same course with an invasion of Jerusalem and desecration of the temple in Jerusalem. Staying true to near/far prophecy, it would seem highly likely that something very similar will take place to mark the beginning of this unequaled time of *tribulation* upon Earth. We should definitely keep our eyes and ears open to current news surrounding the Middle East, Israel, and Jerusalem.
- If events begin to take place today that are similar to those preceding Titus' invasion of Jerusalem and the desecration of the temple at Jerusalem, should we also consider heading for the hills to avoid the coming troubles, whatever they may bring? According to Luke 17:28–32, it seems highly likely.

- The gathering or rapture of God's elect happens *immediately after* the unprecedented *tribulation*: According to the Olivet Discourse, this is fact.
- The sign in the sun, moon, and stars signals the *end of the age*: Based on Scripture, this is also fact.

On this last point, consider the following Old Testament passages:

Behold, the day of the Lord comes, cruel, with wrath and fierce anger, to make the land a desolation and to destroy its sinners from it. For the stars of the heavens and their constellations will not give their light; the sun will be dark at its rising, and the moon will not shed its light. I will punish the world for its evil, and the wicked for their iniquity; I will put an end to the pomp of the arrogant, and lay low the pompous pride of the ruthless. I will make people more rare than fine gold, and mankind than the gold of Ophir. Therefore I will make the heavens tremble, and the earth will be shaken out of its place, at the wrath of the Lord of hosts in the day of his fierce anger (Isaiah 13:9–13).

Blow a trumpet in Zion; sound an alarm on my holy mountain! Let all the inhabitants of the land tremble, for the day of the Lord is coming; it is near, a day of darkness and gloom, a day of clouds and thick darkness! Like blackness there is spread upon the mountains a great and powerful people; their like has never been before, nor will be again after them through the years of all generations (Joel 2:1–2).

The earth quakes before them; the heavens tremble. The sun and the moon are darkened, and the stars withdraw their shining. The Lord utters his voice before his army, for his camp is exceedingly great; he who executes his word is powerful. For the day of the Lord is great and very awesome; who can endure it? (Joel 2:10–11)

Multitudes, multitudes, in the valley of decision! For the day of the Lord is near in the valley of decision. The sun and the moon are darkened, and the stars withdraw their shining. The Lord roars from Zion, and utters his voice from Jerusalem, and the heavens and the earth quake. But the Lord is a refuge to his people, a stronghold to the people of Israel (Joel 3:14–16).

The books of Isaiah and Joel deal with both near and far prophesy. However, these particular verses confirm that the signs in the heavens, the sun, the moon, and the stars occur when *the day of the Lord*—the time of the Lord's judgment and the *end of the age* as we know it—is at hand. We also know from the Olivet Discourse that Jesus' return coincides with the same event.

Do you see it? Do you see the sequence? Just to be clear, let us review it one more time.

FIRST: A gradual increase in:

- False Christianity.
- *Wars and rumors of wars.*
- *Famines and earthquakes.*
- Persecution and death for those that truly believe in Jesus.
- Rejection of the Christian faith and resultant betrayal.
- *Love of many* growing cold.

And **WHEN**:

- The temple at Jerusalem is desecrated by the ***abomination of desolation...***
- (See the book of Daniel for further information.)

THEN:

- Comes unparalleled *tribulation* on Earth.
- Do not believe anyone who says they know where the Christ is.
- *False christs and false prophets* will come, performing *great signs and wonders* that could deceive, *if possible, even the elect.*
- It will be obvious when the Son of Man comes.

Immediately **AFTER** this unequaled *tribulation*:

- *Sun will be darkened.*
- *Moon will not give its light.*
- *Stars will fall from the sky.*
- *Powers of the heavens will be shaken.*
- The above signals the *day of the Lord* and His judgment.

AT THE SAME TIME:

- *The sign of the Son of Man* will appear in the sky *as lightning comes from the east and shines as far as the west.*
- All nations *will mourn* and s*ee the Son of Man coming on the clouds of heaven with power and great glory.*
- The Son of Man will send His angels *with a loud trumpet call* and gather His elect from the four corners of heaven and Earth.

Do you see the sequence? Has anyone ever told you differently? Has their argument against this seemed complicated or difficult to understand? Jesus forewarned that *false christs and false prophets* would increasingly abound and attempt to sidetrack us from the simplicity of the truth. Sometimes there are well-intentioned people that want to hold firmly to their beliefs simply because they have always done so despite any contrary evidence.

But what if? What if what Jesus says is true, and in the exact order He outlines? If so, we probably have some work to do.

So far, Jesus has given us some amazing information, together with a warning, but He is not finished. There are still some important points about His return that He wants to relay to His disciples. Understanding their significance could mean the difference between life and death.

It is simply A Matter Of When

Chapter 6

The Olivet Discourse, Part 3
(Matthew 24:32–51)

Those That Believe Are Prayerfully Watching

Our current understanding of end-time prophecy, based on a face value hermeneutic, ranges from what we consider to be fact to what we do not yet know. The gray areas of likelihood and speculation fall somewhere in between. (See **Chapter 5**.) If for no other reason, this lack of total clarity should help those who seek to follow Jesus avoid becoming lazy and complacent. Such attitudes tend to creep in when we think there is nothing more to learn.

God made humanity, and He knows our nature better than anyone. He wants to keep His people alert. To do this, He has left some things about the future cloaked in mystery. This compels us to keep watch. Jesus has plainly outlined the signs to look for, numerous signs that together paint an increasingly clearer picture as the time for His return draws near. If we follow Jesus' advice and refer back to the writings of Daniel, something we will do later, we will see just how lucid this picture becomes. When the stage is set, the clock will start ticking. Then we will know, within a very small margin of possibility, how long it will be to the *end of the age*.

Let us stay with Jesus as He continues describing His return from the heavens, the gathering of His elect, and the coming judgment.

"From the fig tree learn its lesson: as soon as its branch becomes tender and puts out its leaves, you know that summer is near. So also, when you see all these things, you know that he is near, at the very gates. Truly, I say to you, this generation will not pass away until all these things take place. Heaven and earth will pass away, but my words will not pass away" (verses 32–35).

Scholarly discussions surrounding these particular verses provide an excellent example of speculative interpretation when trying to understand some prophetic Scriptures. Israel became a nation in 1948, and the fig tree was named its national symbol. Many scholars thought that this event, along with its fig tree symbolism, might have been what Jesus was alluding to in these verses. They reasoned that the end could very well be within one generation from the founding of the nation of Israel. Although there are varying thoughts as to the duration of a post-flood biblical generation, the range is generally from 35 to 50 years. (Prior to the flood, people lived hundreds of years. See Genesis chapter 5.) Following the above reasoning, this would have placed Jesus' second coming no later than 1998. This obviously did not happen, at least not in the way Jesus described it.

So then, what do these series of verses about the fig tree actually signify? Sticking to our face value method of interpretation, they seem to simply suggest that as the sprouting of new leaves on a fig tree signals the onset of summer, the growing frequency and intensity of the signs He is giving will eventually indicate that His coming is very close at hand, even within one generation. Is there something more to it? At this point any assumptions would be speculative at best.

Ever since Jesus' Olivet Discourse, there have been scholars who believed they were living in the times just prior to His return. Understandably, this is based on the ever-increasing world tensions and atrocities we have experienced over the centuries. But a closer look into all relevant end-time prophetic Scripture reveals certain signs that have not yet happened, ones that will ultimately demonstrate that the final countdown has actually begun. As Jesus indicated, and we will later see, some of these signs are found in the writings of Daniel.

Jesus also declares in verse 35 that *heaven and earth will pass away*, at least as we know them, but His Word will not. We can have full assurance that what Jesus is telling us will come to pass.

"But concerning that day and hour no one knows, not even the angels of heaven, nor the Son, but the Father only" (verse 36).

Such passages are often the subject of doctoral dissertations. One of the more debated topics surrounding this particular verse concerns the extent of Jesus' knowledge while on Earth. Was He only unaware of the day or hour of His return during His earthly ministry? After all, Jesus said, *"I and the Father are one"* (John 10:30). While this has raised some interesting discussion, it is not really relevant for our purposes. Jesus could have easily said during His Olivet Discourse, "Not even the Son knows the day or the hour until He is glorified by the Father." But He did not. The main point is that the Father is not going to openly divulge this information. Those claiming to know the day and hour have led many unwitting and would-be followers astray. The exact timing of Jesus' second coming is not for us to know.

God's mandate is to stay alert and carefully *watch* for the signs His Son has given.

"For as were the days of Noah, so will be the coming of the Son of Man. For as in those days before the flood they were eating and drinking, marrying and giving in marriage, until the day when Noah entered the ark, and they were unaware until the flood came and swept them all away, so will be the coming of the Son of Man" (verses 37–39).

When Jesus returns, there will only be two groups of people living on Earth:

1. Those that know what is coming, based on God's Word, and have prepared accordingly.
2. Those that do not know what is coming, that do not believe, or that simply do not care and are attempting to live life as normally as possible.

It will be that simple. In the time of Noah, the latter group was made up of every human being except for Noah and his family.

What separated Noah from everyone else? *"Noah found favor in the eyes of the Lord* [and] *was a righteous man, blameless in his generation. Noah walked with God"* (Genesis 6:8, 9b). God also said to Noah, *"I have seen that you are righteous before me in this generation"* (Genesis 7:1b). Yet Scripture also states, *"None is righteous, no, not one; no one understands; no one seeks God. All have turned aside; together they have become worthless; no one does good, not even one"* (Romans 3:10–12, quoting Psalm 14). How, then, could God call Noah righteous? It is summed up in this: *"Abraham believed God, and it was counted to him as righteousness"* (Romans 4:3, Galatians 3:6, James 2:23; emphasis added). We know that Noah believed God because he did all that God commanded him (Genesis 6:22, 7:5).

Throughout Scripture, God highly commends and rewards those that believe on Him and His Word. *"For God so loved the world that he gave his only Son, that whoever believes in him should not perish but have eternal life"* (John 3:16). Believing is not a work of the flesh but an act of faith and confession. It is an admission that we need something beyond our human capability. We have absolutely no righteousness of our own (Isaiah 64:6), but we can claim the true righteousness that comes from God through the amazing work of Christ on the cross. *"For our sake* [God] *made* [Jesus] *to be sin who knew no sin, so that in* [Jesus] *we might become the righteousness of God"* (2 Corinthians 5:21).

As for the believers that came before Jesus, the author of Hebrews says, *"Now faith is the assurance of things hoped for, the conviction of things not seen. For by it the people of old received their commendation"* (Hebrews 11:1–2). The Old Testament saints simply believed in the word that God revealed to them, and through faith in His Word, God called them His own.

> *These all died in faith, not having received the things promised, but having seen them and greeted them from afar ... Therefore God is not ashamed to be called their God, for he has prepared for them a city* (Hebrews 11:13a, 16b).

At the time of the Lord's return, the group of nonbelievers will be quite substantial, just as it was in the days of Noah. Though there will be significantly more believers than just one family who will be prepared and ready for Jesus' second coming, compared to the unbelieving masses, it will be quite small, just as it was before the flood (Genesis chapters 6–7).

In His **Sermon on the Mount**, Jesus told His disciples:

> *"Enter by the narrow gate. For the gate is wide and the way is easy that leads to destruction, and those who enter*

by it are many. For the gate is narrow and the way is hard that leads to life, and those who find it are few" (Matthew 7:13–14).

True believers in Christ have always been in the minority. Continuing with Matthew chapter 24:

"Then two men will be in the field; one will be taken and one left. Two women will be grinding at the mill; one will be taken and one left" (verses 40–41).

Similar in nature, though stated somewhat differently, Luke recounts Jesus' message like this:

"I tell you, in that night there will be two in one bed. One will be taken and the other left. There will be two women grinding together. One will be taken and the other left. Two men will be in the field; one will be taken and the other left" (Luke 17:34–36; verse 36 appears in some manuscripts but not others).

Are the following verses about the gathering of the elect suggesting the rapture, as they are commonly interpreted?

"And he will send out his angels with a loud trumpet call, and they will gather his elect from the four winds, from one end of heaven to the other" (Matthew 24:31).

"And then he will send out the angels and gather his elect from the four winds, from the ends of the earth to the ends of heaven" (Mark 13:27).

For the Lord himself will descend from heaven with a cry of command, with the voice of an archangel, and with the sound of the trumpet of God. And the dead in Christ will rise first. Then we who are alive, who are left, will be caught up together with them in the clouds to meet the Lord in the air, and so we will always be with the Lord (1 Thessalonians 4:16–17).

Or are they about something else? Let us examine the context of both Matthew 24:40–41 and Luke 17:34–36 more closely.

In Matthew 24 so far, Jesus has told His disciples:

- About the signs preceding His coming.
- To head for the hills at the appearance of the **abomination of desolation**.
- The worst *tribulation* ever will engulf the earth.
- Only after this *tribulation* period will His elect be gathered.
- It will be like it was in *the days of Noah* around the time of His coming.
- People will be attempting to live life normally and will be totally unaware of the coming *tribulation*.

Afterwards Jesus states:

"*Then two men will be in the field; one will be taken and one left. Two women will be grinding at the mill; one will be taken and one left*" (verses 40–41).

Jesus does not directly indicate where the *one will be taken* or who is the *one left*.

Let us look at the context.

In the passage immediately preceding verses 40 and 41 of Matthew 24, Jesus is talking about the days of Noah and his preparation *before the flood* that resulted in everyone other than Noah and his family being swept away. So, is Jesus talking about the gathering of His elect or the time immediately before? Let us go back to the story of the flood.

What happened with Noah in his day? God warned Noah in advance of the coming flood. What did Noah do as a result?

By faith Noah, being warned by God concerning events as yet unseen, in reverent fear constructed an ark for the saving of his household (Hebrews 11:7a).

Noah believed God, heeded His warning, obeyed His instructions, and built *an ark for the saving of his household.* Noah and his family survived. All those left behind—whether in bed, in the field, or at the mill—perished during the flood.

So then, who is being *taken* and who will be *left* behind—and where—according to Matthew 24:40–41?

Following the story of Noah, it is possible to imagine that some of Noah's family could have been *working in the field* and *grinding at the mill* alongside others in their community during the course of an average day. Though the main focus of Noah's family might have been maintaining the patriarch's property, some could have been laboring in other fields or mills as an additional source of income. Today, believers and nonbelievers frequently work side by side. But once God spoke to Noah about the coming flood, it is likely that this scenario would have dramatically changed. There was work to be done according to God's command to prepare an ark. Based on God's instructions to Noah, it would seem that Noah and his family were being separated or *taken* by God to prepare for the impending flood of God's judgment. The unbelievers were being *left* to their own fate.

After Jesus compares the time of His return to the days of Noah, Luke adds this from Jesus' discourse:

"Likewise, just as it was in the days of Lot—they were eating and drinking, buying and selling, planting and building, but on the day when Lot went out from Sodom, fire and sulfur rained from heaven and destroyed them all—so will it be on the day when the Son of Man is revealed. On that day, let the one who is on the housetop, with his goods in the house, not come down to take them away, and likewise let the one who is in the field not turn back. Remember Lot's wife" (Luke 17:28–32).

If verses 40 and 41 of Matthew are about the gathering of the elect, as mentioned in Matthew 24:31, Mark 13:27, and 1 Thessalonians 4:16–17, then there would be no reason to even consider going back home to get anything. The *elect* would be taken to be with Jesus in the heavens. Lot and his family were not taken into heaven but were told to "get out of town!" Jesus similarly told His disciples that when they begin to see all the signs He is mentioning, they should also take off and not look back (Matthew 24:15–18).

Concerning Lot's situation, the book of Genesis states:

As morning dawned, the angels urged Lot, saying, "Up! Take your wife and your two daughters who are here, lest you be swept away in the punishment of the city." But he lingered. So the men seized him and his wife and his two daughters by the hand, the Lord being merciful to him, and they brought him out and set him outside the city. And as they brought them out, one said, "Escape for your life. Do not look back or stop anywhere in the valley. Escape to the hills, lest you be swept away" (Genesis 19:15–17).

However, Lot's wife failed to follow God's warning:

Then the Lord rained on Sodom and Gomorrah sulfur and fire from the Lord out of heaven. And he overthrew those cities, and all the valley, and all the inhabitants of the cities, and what grew on the ground. But Lot's wife, behind him, looked back, and she became a pillar of salt (Genesis 19:24–26).

Lot and his family were *taken* from the impending calamities. Though Lot appeared to dawdle, God had mercy and *the angels* dragged him and his family out of town. The only remaining instruction: do not stop or look back. The message in the Olivet Discourse bears the same advice.

Jesus has already told us that it will only be *after the tribulation of those days* when He will gather His elect, not before

(Matthew 24:21,31). At face value, it would appear that those alive during this time will have to face this *tribulation*. But as God did with Noah, Jesus wants to prepare His disciples beforehand so that when certain signs unfold, they will know to get out of town fast—and not look back. He knows what is coming will be the worst period of *tribulation* the world has ever seen (Matthew 24:15–22). The context of verses 40 and 41 in Matthew indicate a forewarning along with the need for preparation and compliance.

Let us consider Noah and his family once again.

As the time of the flood drew near, do you think any of them were working *side by side* with those about to perish? It would seem more plausible that they were working *in the field* and *grinding a hand mill* to prepare food for their own journey, along with loading it into the ark in obedience to God before the floods came.

> *"Also take with you every sort of food that is eaten, and store it up. It shall serve as food for you and for them." Noah did this; he did all that God commanded him* (Genesis 6:21–22).

The rest of humanity was certainly not preparing provisions for any floating escape vessel. They were in fields and grinding at mills for their own earthly sustenance, oblivious to the fact that they were living in disobedience to God and would soon perish. It is more realistic to assume that those closely following God's Word as Jesus' return approaches will not be working side by side with those who are in rebellion. Their goals and direction will be extremely different.

There are many who have attempted to use verses 40 and 41 of Matthew 24 about one being *taken* and another *left* to prove that the gathering of the elect will occur prior to any *tribulation* period and during a time of relative peace when believers and nonbelievers are still working together. Yet this interpretation is not in keeping with what Jesus has already stated earlier in verses 29 through 31 (together with Mark 13:27) about the coming ***great tribulation*** or the immediate context of comparison with the days of Noah.

Though God did not tell Noah what day or hour the flood would occur, He did warn Noah it was coming and that he needed to plan accordingly. There was work to do. Therefore, the flood came as no surprise to Noah. He and his family were ready. Does this mean they were *taken*, or chosen by God, to prepare for the coming judgment? Those who know Jesus and understand His Word will follow the directions He has given, just like Noah. The rest of humanity will be *left* behind and met with confusion and chaos.

Let us now look at the verses in Luke that are similar to those in Matthew 24:40–41.

"I tell you, in that night there will be two in one bed. One will be taken and the other left. There will be two women grinding together. One will be taken and the other left. Two men will be in the field; one will be taken and the other left" (Luke 17:34–36; verse 36 appears in some manuscripts but not others).

Once again, the immediate context equates the time of Jesus' return with the times of Noah and Lot. The warning in both cases is to "get out of town" before disaster strikes. In verse 31, Luke quotes Jesus as saying:

"On that day, let the one who is on the housetop, with his goods in the house, not come down to take them away, and likewise let the one who is in the field not turn back."

Matthew puts the context of this verse at the placing of the ***abomination of desolation***, initiating what is known as the ***great tribulation*** (Matthew 24:15, 21 KJV). It is only after this *tribulation* that Jesus returns and gathers His elect.

So what about the one *taken* and the one *left* in the case of Luke 17:34–36?

In Luke's account of this section, there are two in one bed and two women grinding together, with one being *taken* and the other *left* in each case. If this is not talking about the gathering of the elect, then—once again—where is the one *taken* going, and who is the one that is *left?* As we will see in the coming parables of Matthew chapter 25, not everyone who claims to believe in Jesus actually knows His will. Is it possible that within the Christian community some will be ready and willing to follow Jesus' instructions while others will not, even among immediate family members? Will this result in some being *taken* to prepare or flee, as with Noah and Lot, while others choose not to follow and are *left* behind? What do you see?

The final verse in Luke chapter 17 says:

"And they said to him, 'Where, Lord?' He said to them, 'Where the corpse is, there the vultures will gather'" (Luke 17:37).

As opposed to Matthew 24:28, where the use of "corpse" and "vultures" seem appropriate according to the original word usage, here the Greek indicates a live body rather than a dead one. In this case, the King James Version seems more appropriate:

"And they answered and said unto him, Where, Lord? And he said unto them, Wheresoever the body is, thither will the eagles be gathered together".

This body is alive. The *eagles* will *be gathered* to it. Those living in Jesus will follow Him and Him alone.

But they who wait for the Lord shall renew their strength; they shall mount up with wings like eagles; they shall run and not be weary; they shall walk and not faint (Isaiah 40:31).

From the overall context of the passages above, it would seem that those being *taken* are making necessary preparations ahead of the impending ***great tribulation*** in accordance with Jesus' admonitions and warnings. Those closely following Jesus, and in tune with His Word, will be obedient to His instructions. The unbelieving are *left* behind wherever they may be. (Consider Matthew 19:29 for perspective.)

Do you see it differently?

Do you see these verses as indicating that the rapture, or the Lord's gathering of the saints, will suddenly come *as a thief in the night* before any major calamity engulfs Earth? If you do, I urge you to go back and review the context of verses 40 and 41 in Matthew and seriously consider what Jesus has already put forth in His Olivet Discourse. I would just caution you to beware of falling into the trap of taking any of these verses out of context to justify a position that may prove erroneous and potentially dangerous. Failure to understand and accurately follow Jesus' instructions could prove quite costly.

Returning to the Olivet Discourse in Matthew chapter 24:

"Therefore, stay awake, for you do not know on what day your Lord is coming. But know this, that if the master of the house had known in what part of the night the thief was coming, he would have stayed awake and would not have let his house be broken into. Therefore you also must be ready, for the Son of Man is coming at an hour you do not expect" (verses 42–44).

Jesus reiterates that we will not know the day or hour of His return. At the same time, He also admonishes us to know *in what part of the night the thief* [is] *coming*. This may indicate that the signs Jesus is giving will help us approximate the general time of His arrival so that our *house* [will not] *be broken into* as we prepare for more specific signs to be revealed. The sequence of events Jesus outlines, together with information about His second coming found elsewhere in Scripture, will help us do just this.

For you yourselves are fully aware that the day of the Lord will come like a thief in the night. While people are saying, "There is peace and security," then sudden destruction will come upon them as labor pains come upon a pregnant woman, and they will not escape. But you are not in darkness, brothers, for that day to surprise you like a thief (1 Thessalonians 5:2–4).

But the day of the Lord will come like a thief, and then the heavens will pass away with a roar, and the heavenly bodies will be burned up and dissolved, and the earth and the works that are done on it will be exposed (2 Peter 3:10).

"Remember, then, what you received and heard. Keep it, and repent. If you will not wake up, I will come like a thief, and you will not know at what hour I will come against you" (Revelation 3:3).

"Behold, I am coming like a thief! Blessed is the one who stays awake, keeping his garments on, that he may not go about naked and be seen exposed!" (Revelation 16:15)

We do not know the day or hour, but if we faithfully watch for the signs Jesus is giving—and prepare accordingly—His coming will not catch us off guard *like a thief.* This is His promise, and His Word does not fail.

"Who then is the faithful and wise servant, whom his master has set over his household, to give them their food at the proper time? Blessed is that servant whom his master will find so doing when he comes. Truly, I say to you, he will set him over all his possessions. But if that wicked servant says to himself, 'My master is delayed,' and begins to beat his fellow servants and eats and drinks with drunkards, the master of that servant will come on a day when he does not expect him and at an hour he does not know and will cut him in pieces and put him with the hypocrites. In that place there will be weeping and gnashing of teeth" (verses 45–51).

One of the greatest criticisms of the Christian church at large is the obvious hypocrisy frequently witnessed among its members. Professing Christians too often say one thing, yet do the opposite. The term "Christian" has become muddied and nearly meaningless. For this reason, a more appropriate term for those sincerely seeking Jesus' guidance through His Word might be Christ-followers. The passage above provides a perfect case in point.

Jesus separates *the faithful and wise servant*s from the *wicked* ones. Following the context, the wise servants are feeding their fellow servants in Jesus' household with His words of truth as they watch for the signs of His coming. The wicked servants have lost faith and are failing to either watch or help their fellow servants do the same.

The fact that the wicked servant—

- *Beat his fellow servants.*
- Began to *eat and drink with drunkards.*
- And was *cut to pieces and put with the hypocrites, where there will be weeping and gnashing of teeth.*

—seems to indicate that these wicked servants were never really one of His elect in the first place.

This should serve as an ominous warning. To remain faithful means to stay true and stand firm. The result of deviation, according to Jesus' description above, is fatal.

There are many different reactions from those who hear the Word of God. In the parable of the sower, as recounted in Matthew chapter 13, Jesus breaks it down into four basic categories:

1. Those who hear about the kingdom but do not understand it. Then Satan *comes and snatches away what was sown in* [their hearts]. (verse 19)

2. *Those who* [hear] *the word and immediately* [receive] *it with joy, yet* [have] *no root* [within], *but* [endure] *for a while, and when tribulation or persecution arises on account of the word, immediately* [they fall] *away.* (verse 20–21)
3. *As for what was sown among thorns,* [these are] *the* [ones] *who* [hear] *the word, but the cares of the world and the deceitfulness of riches choke the word, and it proves unfruitful.* (verse 22)
4. *Those who* [hear] *the word and* [understand] *it.* [They] *indeed* [bear] *fruit and yield, in one case a hundredfold, in another sixty, and in another thirty.* (verse 23)

The *faithful and wise servant* Jesus mentions in Matthew 24:45–47 clearly falls into category four from the parable of the sower. The other three fall short.

Knowing the future, and the deceitfulness of the human heart (Jeremiah 17:9), Jesus is not done painting the picture for His disciples of what is to come when He returns. He loves to tell stories and parables to make His point. Some who hear them will understand; others will not. Those that fall into category four from the parable of the sower will understand.

Do we truly believe in Him? Do we believe what He says about His coming? Have we eliminated our filters and prejudices so that we understand exactly what He is telling us?

This brings us to the end of Matthew chapter 24. Matthew chapter 25 contains the remaining portion of Jesus' Olivet Discourse as recounted by Matthew. It begins with two more parables or stories. The first one paints a vivid picture of the mindset Jesus expects us to have as we prepare for His return. In this parable Jesus seems to be asking the following question: Will we be fully prepared to meet Him should His return be a long time in coming and in the dark? (Matthew 25:5) If not, we may be left where *there will be weeping and gnashing of teeth.*

Chapter 7

The Olivet Discourse, Part 4
(Matthew 25:1–13; the Parable of the Ten Virgins)

Do You Have Enough Oil?

We are coming down the homestretch of Jesus' Olivet Discourse. So far He has outlined a very specific order of events that will precede and surround His second coming. He has told us that the increasing intensity of these events will be like a woman's labor during childbearing. Though initially intermittent and relatively mild, the labor pains will ultimately surge in frequency and intensity. He has also warned us time and again to *watch* because no one knows the day or hour of His coming. This idea of keeping watch has interesting significance when comparing the first disciples' generation to that of ours.

What do you suppose Jesus' original followers took notice of in their day? Loved ones laboring hours to prepare meals from sometimes scarce or limited resources? Maybe people in open marketplaces buying, selling, and trading local and imported goods? Children playing in parks and streets? Numerous camel trains of travelers, both familiar and foreign, coming and going through the city gates? This is all very likely. How about large numbers of converts being added daily to the church (Acts 2:47)? Yes, that too. In stark contrast, they may also have kept an eye out for Roman soldiers searching for those fanatical Christians who were attempting to turn the world upside down with their new message and subvert the status quo. And then there were the jealous religious leaders who desperately wanted to put an end to this sect that was proselytizing their followers (John 12:19; Acts 24:5, 28:22).

What tends to be the focus of our generation is very different. Our eyes are lulled by every medium available to gaze upon the myriad of enticing things the world has to offer. In the years to come, the global marketplace will grow exponentially in both size and availability. What draws our attention? Fashion? Luxury? Stardom? Sensuality? Royalty? The rich and the famous? The latest? The greatest? Sports? What do we watch and why? This is an important question. It is one we should ask ourselves regularly.

How do we spend our time, and what are we looking for? If we are not paying close attention to the right things, we could easily be caught off guard and unprepared for Jesus' return.

Before we take a look at the first parable of Matthew chapter 25, let us consider why Jesus used parables.

In Mark 4:10–12, after Jesus introduced the parable of the sower, He was alone with His disciples when someone asked Him about His parables. Jesus answered,

"To you has been given the secret of the kingdom of God, but for those outside everything is in parables, so that 'they may indeed see but not perceive, and may indeed hear but not understand, lest they should turn and be forgiven.'"
(Jesus is referencing Isaiah 6:9.)

Jesus uses parables to draw to Himself those that the Father has called, while confounding all who are apathetic to His teaching. True believers hear His voice, follow Him, and understand His words (John 6:44, 10:27).

With this short explanation in place, let us take a look at the *parable of the ten virgins*.

"Then the kingdom of heaven will be like ten virgins who took their lamps and went to meet the bridegroom. Five of them were foolish, and five were wise. For when the foolish took their lamps, they took no oil with them, but the wise took flasks of oil with their lamps" (Matthew 25:1–4).

Continuing to instruct His disciples, Jesus begins the parable of the ten virgins with *"Then,"* or as translated in the NIV, *"At that time."* What time? Look at the context. Jesus is still talking about His second coming. And whom is He talking about? The text indicates that all ten virgins are preparing for the arrival of the bridegroom. This is not a story about nonbelievers but about those claiming to follow Jesus. All ten are fully aware of the bridegroom's coming and have every intention of meeting him when he arrives. But there is a slight problem. Jesus says only half of them are fully prepared. Let us take a closer look.

"For when the foolish took their lamps, they took no oil with them, but the wise took flasks of oil with their lamps" (Matthew 25:3–4).

What do you see? Though all ten virgins brought lamps in preparation for meeting the bridegroom, it seems only five thought they might actually need their lamps for an extended period of time. Are these five anticipating a potentially longer journey, one that might require navigating their way in the dark, and so they carried extra oil?

What is the overall preparedness of the ten virgins?

1. Know the bridegroom is coming. Check.
2. Carry a lamp in case light is needed for their journey. Check.
3. Have extra oil on hand should their wait be long or their journey continue deep into the night. Half check. According to Jesus, only five of the ten are ready for this last scenario.

> *"As the bridegroom was delayed, they all became drowsy and slept. But at midnight there was a cry, 'Here is the bridegroom! Come out to meet him.' Then all those virgins rose and trimmed their lamps. And the foolish said to the wise, 'Give us some of your oil, for our lamps are going out.' But the wise answered, saying, 'Since there will not be enough for us and for you, go rather to the dealers and buy for yourselves.' And while they were going to buy, the bridegroom came, and those who were ready went in with him to the marriage feast, and the door was shut. Afterward the other virgins came also, saying, 'Lord, lord, open to us.' But he answered, 'Truly, I say to you, I do not know you.' Watch therefore, for you know neither the day nor the hour"* (Matthew 25:5–13).

Jesus has already told us that tumultuous times will increase before His second coming. If we take Him at His word, He also states that we are going to pass through a time of **great tribulation** just prior to His return (Matthew 24:21, Mark 13:19). With this in mind, what do you see that divides the five foolish virgins from the five wise virgins?

First, what are the similarities between the ten virgins?

- They are all awaiting the arrival of the bridegroom.
- They all understand that they might need a lamp for their journey.

- They all become *drowsy* and fall *asleep*.
- At midnight they all hear the *cry* that the bridegroom has arrived and are summoned to meet him.
- They all know that they must *trim* their lamps to safely navigate their way, as it is now dark.

The similarities end here, and the singular difference is enough for the bridegroom to say to the five foolish virgins, *"I do not know you."* The foolish five suddenly realize they are running out of oil and might not have enough to complete their journey. Faced with this ominous reality, they ask the five wise virgins to give them some of their oil. From here the story takes a significant turn.

Those anxiously awaiting Jesus' second coming obviously consider themselves Christians and part of the bride of Christ. And practicing Christians are generally known for their generosity, right? Yes. In this situation, however, Jesus paints a very different picture.

When the foolish virgins ask the wise ones for help, they reply, *"Since there will not be enough for us and for you, go rather to the dealers and buy for yourselves."* The two groups are now heading in opposite directions. The five wise and prepared virgins soon enter into the banquet at the bridegroom's arrival. When the five foolish and unprepared virgins finally show up, they are left outside. The banquet door has been shut. They are simply told by the bridegroom, *"I do not know you."*

What do you think Jesus is telling His followers here? Is only being somewhat prepared going to be good enough? It appears that a significant number of those professing to be Jesus' followers will not gain admission to the wedding banquet at His return. Why? Since they are not fully prepared, they fail to arrive on time and ultimately face a closed door. They come up short. Those who are prepared, according to the parable, will not have enough to share with those that are not lest they both end up late when He arrives.

Does this seem harsh? Why would Jesus, the physical incarnation of the one and only true God, reject those that apparently believe on Him just because they did not have enough oil? The answer is not that complicated.

Suppose you were medically diagnosed with a condition requiring major surgery. Who would you select to be your physician? A well-known and highly rated specialist who has done the necessary homework and thoroughly studied or someone who is simply "winging it" based on what is hoped to be the best approach? Just as the best and most qualified doctors put in the time and effort to thoroughly learn their profession, so should those endeavoring to correctly understand the Bible. Scripture is not as complicated as you might think, but it does require personal study.

This is the dilemma, one we have been addressing from the beginning. None of our beliefs about the end times or any other biblical topic should be based on what someone else has told us or on what we wish to believe. This is not about us. This is about God's plan for humanity. Where do we discover this plan? It is all in His Word, and it is not meant to be a stretch of our imagination. Though some things are concealed until the appropriate time, there is a significant amount of critical information He is revealing to us now. There is so much we can understand if we actually read His Word and take it at face value.

What reasonable assumptions can we make about the parable of the ten virgins?

- The ten virgins are like those who claim to follow Jesus, know He is returning, and have made preparations according to their individual beliefs.

- The five wise virgins are like those among Jesus' followers who are prepared for a potentially long or dark journey till He arrives.
- The five foolish virgins are like those followers who appear to envision a shorter journey and only have minimal provision.
- Jesus' coming will probably seem *delayed* or near *midnight* when He arrives.
- The *wise* followers, who have prepared for a longer journey, will not be able to share their resources with the *foolish* ones who have not sufficiently prepared lest no one complete the journey.
- Jesus ultimately tells the unprepared that He does not know them.

Jesus begins the parable of the ten virgins, the first of His concluding stories, with *"At that time"* (NIV) of His return. In the context of the story, His return is fast approaching. He knows that what His professing followers actually believe will determine how they prepare for His arrival.

What do you believe? What will you do? How will you prepare? Will it be based only on what you have heard? Will it be based on novels, commentaries, church doctrine, some movie you have seen, or what you personally expect or hope God to do? The best place to start your analysis is with His Word and not someone else's ideas, including mine. I only want to inspire you to seek out the truth for yourself. All I am doing here is laying out a systematic commentary; it is up to you to decide what is right based on your own diligent study.

If you are reading this book, you probably live in the free world where it is not illegal to own or read a Bible—at least not yet. Hopefully we will each cherish this privilege and choose to use our freedom wisely.

This brings us to the parable of the talents, Jesus' final parable in His Olivet Discourse. What will we do with the treasure we have been given from the Master?

Chapter 8

The Olivet Discourse Part 5
(Matthew 25:18–30; the Parable of the Talents)

Have You Invested Wisely?

Jesus does not mince words as He nears the conclusion of His discourse. He knows He will soon be put to death and that time is running short. He still has some important things to share with His disciples before He is betrayed and handed over to be crucified. One of these final messages is found in the *parable of the talents*. In this story, Jesus underscores the importance He places on sharing His Word with others. For those who do, the rewards are great. For those who bury His Word for whatever reason, it will prove costly.

In the parable of the ten virgins, covered in **Chapter 7**, Jesus seems to say that:

- We understand what He is saying and are prepared accordingly, or we do not and are not.
- We know Him and are known by Him, or we do not and are not.

- We will either enter in to be with Him when He arrives, or we will be left out.

In the parable of the talents, Jesus takes this one step further. He explains to His disciples the seriousness of wisely investing all that He has given them. One servant in the story failed miserably because he neither knew his master nor understood his will. We should each pray earnestly to avoid this same error—and its end result.

"For it will be like a man going on a journey, who called his servants and entrusted to them his property. To one he gave five talents, to another two, to another one, to each according to his ability. Then he went away. He who had received the five talents went at once and traded with them, and he made five talents more. So also he who had the two talents made two talents more. But he who had received the one talent went and dug in the ground and hid his master's money" (Matthew 25:14–18).

Who do you believe is the *man going on a journey*? Let us examine the context.

Jesus has not changed subjects. He is still instructing His disciples about His return and the coming judgment. Therefore we can reasonably assume the man is Jesus and that we are the servants among whom He is dividing His *property* during His absence.

Similar to the parable of the ten virgins, this story is presumably about professing Christians rather than nonbelievers as all three servants are members of the master's household. Jesus knew He would soon be making His journey back to the heavenly realms. His *property* is His Word. Not only is His Word truth (John 8:31–32), but it is through His Word that all things exist and are sustained (Genesis 1:3–31; Psalm 33:6; 2 Peter 3:5; Hebrews 1:3). In this particular case, He is entrusting His household of disciples with this amazing insight into the final period of current world history. Jesus' desire is to reap long-term dividends as His disciples share this incredible revelation with others. Just as Jesus invested in His disciples, He wants His future followers to invest in others by proclaiming this end-time gospel of the kingdom.

In the story, two of the three servants immediately went to work and doubled what their master had given them. The last servant simply hid what he had received.

"Now after a long time the master of those servants came and settled accounts with them. And he who had received the five talents came forward, bringing five talents more, saying, 'Master, you delivered to me five talents; here I have made five talents more.' His master said to him, 'Well done, good and faithful servant. You have been faithful over a little; I will set you over much. Enter into the joy of your master.' And he also who had the two talents came forward, saying, 'Master, you delivered to me two talents; here I have made two talents more.' His master said to him, 'Well done, good and faithful servant. You have been faithful over a little; I will set you over much. Enter into the joy of your master'" (Matthew 25:19–23).

The master highly commended his two diligent servants. He rewarded them with considerably more because of their faithfulness *over a little*. The third servant received a very different reaction from the master.

"He also who had received the one talent came forward, saying, 'Master, I knew you to be a hard man, reaping where you did not sow, and gathering where you scattered no seed, so I was afraid, and I went and hid your talent in the ground. Here you have what is yours.' But his master answered him, 'You wicked and slothful servant! You knew

that I reap where I have not sown and gather where I scattered no seed? Then you ought to have invested my money with the bankers, and at my coming I should have received what was my own with interest.

"'So take the talent from him and give it to him who has the ten talents. For to everyone who has will more be given, and he will have an abundance. But from the one who has not, even what he has will be taken away. And cast the worthless servant into the outer darkness. In that place there will be weeping and gnashing of teeth'" (Matthew 25:24–30).

The master was furious with the servant who hid his talent in a hole and handed it back "as is" when the master returned. But what may not be so apparent is equally important. What is the servant's excuse for burying his master's money?

"Master, I knew you to be a hard man, reaping where you did not sow, and gathering where you scattered no seed, so I was afraid, and I went and hid your talent in the ground."

Is the wicked servant's evaluation of his master accurate? Context is everything. If the *master* represents Jesus, as the story suggests, this third servant's assessment of his master is totally misguided. Then why would Jesus put this in the story? The clarity comes when Jesus states the master's response to his servant's excuse.

"You wicked and slothful servant! You knew that I reap where I have not sown and gather where I scattered no seed? Then you ought to have invested my money with the bankers, and at my coming I should have received what was my own with interest."

If the servant had been correct in his analysis of his master, the master would not have been justified in calling him either *wicked* or *slothful*. *"You knew…?"* seems more of a shocked amazement by the master than anything else. The master is basically saying to his servant, "You thought that? Really? After all the time you have been with me? But if you actually believed this, then you should have given the money to a banker who could have at least done something with it rather than nothing at all. What were you thinking?"

Why does the master call this servant *wicked*? That is a strong term for one who was entrusted with part of his master's personal wealth. There is no indication in the story of any issues between the master and this servant before. What happened? What do you think? What do you see?

- All three were servants of the master.
- All three were entrusted with varying portions of the master's property.
- All three had the opportunity to do something with the property they were given by the master.
- Two of the servants chose to invest their master's property.
- The third chose to bury it.

It is obvious that something is missing, some sort of relational breakdown between the third servant and his master. It actually seems this servant did not know his master very well at all. Otherwise he would have known what to do with his master's property.

Which of the servants does your life reflect? How well do you know *the Master*? Is it more of an "I will call you if I need you" type of casual and distant relationship that so many professing Christians maintain, one that is primarily based on an intellectual knowledge of God's existence? Or is it something more intimate, centered around a personal study of God's Word together with times of prayer and quiet reflection as you listen for His *still small voice*? (1 Kings

19:12 KJV) The latter group will have obvious reward both in this life and at Jesus' return. Those in the former group may still be in jeopardy.

Many who believe they are living close to God, yet carry the baggage of what they "think" God's Word says, are risking the fate of the five foolish virgins. This is not a judgment. It is what Jesus plainly outlines throughout His discourse. He loves us enough to tell us the truth and warn us of the consequences for adhering to anything other than His Word. It has been this way since Adam and Eve in the garden (Genesis chapters 2–3). Those who sincerely seek to know God, and who are doing their best to eliminate any preconceived notions about Him that might cloud the heart and mind, are following the path Jesus knows is best. All the rest are prone to suffer the sad fate of the *wicked* servant.

Why does the master also call the wicked servant *slothful?* What did the master expect his servants to do? Let us analyze.

Which is easier: Bury the master's property and simply walk away with your own thoughts about the master or wisely invest what the master has given you? Prudent investment takes both time and effort, not something the *slothful* would enjoy—especially if you are not convinced of the real value of the master's property.

Judas Iscariot, one of Jesus' original disciples, was very much like the wicked servant in the parable. Just as the wicked servant misunderstood his master, Judas never understood Jesus' purpose on Earth, even though Judas followed Him for nearly three and a half years. Judas was right there—full-time—with Jesus. Just think about this for a minute.

Other than being known as the one who betrayed Jesus, the disciples referred to Judas as a thief (John 12:5–6). There are no indications in Scripture that Judas actually did anything else, much less something of value, as a disciple.

Judas misused the group finances for his own greedy purposes. Then he allowed his misguided aspirations about the Messiah to blind him to the truth. This ultimately caused Judas to fall prey to Satan and betray Jesus for thirty pieces of silver (Matthew 26:6–16, John 13:18–26).

Judas may have been from an extreme camp of Zealots called Sicarii, or assassins. His name, Iscariot, has been traced to an Aramaic rendering of the word Sikarios, for people from the region of Kerioth-hezron. If he were actually a Zealot, Judas would have been accustomed to listening to others with thoughts just like his. The Zealots were extremely disgruntled with Roman rule. Judas could have easily become caught up in their rhetoric against the treacherous authority of Rome. "Rome is suffocating us! Enough is enough. If the Messiah is coming, He will surely liberate Israel from this unbearable Roman tyranny!" This may have been right in line with what Judas wanted.

But here is the issue, one we have been alluding to from the beginning. This was not about Judas then, and it is not about us today. It is about God and what He has planned for humanity. Whether we agree with Him or not, God knows what is best. Obviously, not everyone likes this idea. Just check the news and an abundance of lawsuits attempting to separate the Judeo-Christian worldview from virtually everything. What Jesus has said in His Olivet Discourse is already coming to pass.

Once Judas realized that what he had vainly pursued was horribly wrong, it was too late. Is this reminiscent of the five foolish virgins and the foolish servant? The damage was done. Judas' own hopes and ambitions were totally false and worthless. Jesus was the prophesied Messiah and had come to do something far beyond Judas' corrupted imagination. In the end, what happened to Judas? He was left outside, *"In that place* [where] *there will be weeping and gnashing of teeth"* (Matthew 25:30, 27:3–5).

As it is with the master in the parable of the talents, Jesus will be just as amazed with any of His followers today who decide to keep this message to themselves or hide it in a hole because they have their own ideas about what is right. Do we know the true Master and understand who He is and what He wants? Or do we have some false perception about Him—just like the wicked and slothful servant did about his master—that will keep us on the sidelines rendering us useless or, worse yet, in serious trouble? What reasonable assumptions can we make about the parable of the talents?

- Like the master in the story who leaves on a long journey, Jesus is speaking of His own journey from Earth back to the heavenly realms and His subsequent return.
- As the master entrusted his property to his servants with the expectation that it would be handled wisely and reap dividends, Jesus is entrusting us with this revelation of His return and the coming judgment, hoping we will share it with others and raise everyone's awareness.
- Similar to how the master *settled accounts* with his *servants* after he returned from his long journey, Jesus will do the same when He returns.
- Those of Jesus' followers who have faithfully spread the message of this gospel will be met with praise and reward, just like the master rewarded his wise servants.
- Jesus' followers with misguided ideas about Him, and who keep His Word and revelation to themselves for whatever reason, will be met with stiff rebuke and cast aside.

- As it was with the five foolish virgins who were left outside the bridegroom's banquet because they were unprepared for his coming, so it was with the wicked and slothful servant who did not truly know his master and hid what the master had given him.

Jesus knows that Satan is going to do everything within his power *to lead astray, if possible, even the elect.* For this reason, He told His disciples earlier, *"See, I have told you beforehand"* (Matthew 24:24b–25). We will have no excuses. Forewarned is forearmed. Have Jesus' words been sufficient warning for you?

It would seem that Jesus wants His followers to fully understand what He has told them and, in turn, share His message with all those they can. To do this successfully they must first listen to His words and accept them at face value. What do you think? Do you see it differently? If so, why?

Jesus told two parables to His disciples near the conclusion of His discourse, stories that paint a rather straightforward picture of what He expects and what is at stake. The rewards are great for all who are ready and willing to take action in accordance with His Word. Those with ideas of their own are apparently left out.

Jesus has one final message to share. It is not a parable. It is not an allegory. He tells His disciples the very simple yet sobering criteria that He will use to judge all the nations *"when* [he] *comes in his glory, and all the angels with him"* (Matthew 25:31a).

Are you ready? At this point there is still time to prepare.

It is simply A Matter Of When

Chapter 9

The Olivet Discourse Part 6
(Matthew 25:31–46; the Sheep and the Goats)

Have You Done the Master's Will or Your Own?

Jesus has one final story to share before concluding His Olivet Discourse. To accurately interpret its meaning, we must correctly identify the scriptural context.

So far there has been a consistent pattern throughout the discourse. Let us recall in Matthew chapter 24 how Jesus systematically walks us through what it will be like before and during the time of His second coming. In the two parables that follow, contained in Matthew chapter 25, Jesus makes vivid distinctions between those who claim to follow Him and those who actually do. Both groups call Him *Lord* or *Master*. However, Jesus indicates that it is only those who truly know Him, and do His will, that are known by Him. These are the ones that are properly preparing for His return and are greatly rewarded for their obedience. For the other group, the consequences are devastating. As you read this final story, see if you can determine if Jesus is continuing to make distinctions between His followers or if there is something else He is teaching us.

Matthew 25:31–46; the sheep and the goats:

"*When the Son of Man comes in his glory, and all the angels with him, then he will sit on his glorious throne. Before him will be gathered all the nations, and he will separate people one from another as a shepherd separates the sheep from the goats. And he will place the sheep on his right, but the goats on the left. Then the King will say to those on his right, 'Come, you who are blessed by my Father, inherit the kingdom prepared for you from the foundation of the world. For I was hungry and you gave me food, I was thirsty and you gave me drink, I was a stranger and you welcomed me, I was naked and you clothed me, I was sick and you visited me, I was in prison and you came to me.' Then the righteous will answer him, saying, 'Lord, when did we see you hungry and feed you, or thirsty and give you drink? And when did we see you a stranger and welcome you, or naked and clothe you? And when did we see you sick or in prison and visit you?' And the King will answer them, 'Truly, I say to you, as you did it to one of the least of these my brothers, you did it to me.'"*

"*Then he will say to those on his left, 'Depart from me, you cursed, into the eternal fire prepared for the devil and his angels. For I was hungry and you gave me no food, I was thirsty and you gave me no drink, I was a stranger and you did not welcome me, naked and you did not clothe me, sick and in prison and you did not visit me.' Then they also will answer, saying, 'Lord, when did we see you hungry or thirsty or a stranger or naked or sick or in prison, and did not minister to you?' Then he will answer them, saying, 'Truly, I say to you, as you did not do it to one of the least of these, you did not do it to me.' And these will go away into eternal punishment, but the righteous into eternal life."*

What do you see? According to the story, Jesus will judge *the nations* when He returns. When it says, *"All nations will be gathered before him,"* many assumptions could be made about what *the nations* represents and which judgment Jesus is speaking of. But since the prior two stories appear to be addressing those who profess to know Jesus, a strong case could be made that this final story is directed toward the church as well. When considering the context and flow of Jesus' overall message throughout His discourse, this would seem more plausible than trying to associate it with something like the Great White Throne Judgment of Revelation chapter 20, which is described very differently.

Both sheep and goats are clean animals according to the Law of Moses, which His disciples would have readily understood (Deuteronomy 14:6). This further lends credence to the idea that Jesus is still talking about those claiming to follow Him. If Jesus was comparing believers with nonbelievers, it makes more sense that He would have chosen an unclean animal, like a pig, to describe nonbelievers rather than a clean one.

(Important note: Though Jesus did many things seemingly contrary to what the religious leaders considered lawful, He lived according to the Law of Moses while on Earth and ultimately fulfilled it [Matthew 5:17]. Being under the law, Jesus spoke in ways His disciples could relate. Jesus also prepared His disciples for some changes that were to come once He completed His earthly ministry. One such change concerned the distinction between clean and unclean animals [Acts 10:1–28]. Jesus knew that after He had fulfilled the law through His perfect sacrifice on the cross, such laws would no longer be necessary [Mark 7:19]. Nevertheless, in light of what Jesus accomplished for our salvation, every believer is now *a temple of the Holy Spirit*. They are not their own but *were bought with a price* and are meant to *glorify God* in their bodies [1 Corinthians 6:19–20]. When we have choices in how we care for our physical bodies, it would seem that doing so in as healthy a manner as possible would better enable us, as His disciples, to do the job of spreading the gospel message.)

Using Scripture to confirm and support other Scripture, and hopefully give us a better understanding of Jesus' message in the sheep and the goats, let us consider some passages that speak further about the attitude and behavior God expects from those who follow Jesus.

In this first passage, Jesus clarifies whom He considers family:

And his mother and his brothers came, and standing outside they sent to him and called him. And a crowd was sitting around him, and they said to him, "Your mother and your brothers are outside, seeking you." And he answered them, "Who are my mother and my brothers?" And looking about at those who sat around him, he said, "Here are my mother and my brothers! For **whoever does the will of God, he is my brother and sister and mother**" (Mark 3:31–35; emphasis added).

Jesus' true family consists of those who do *the will of God*. Consider the following, spoken by the apostle Paul to the Corinthians:

If I speak in the tongues of men and of angels, but have not love, I am a noisy gong or a clanging cymbal. And if I have prophetic powers, and understand all mysteries and all knowledge, and if I have all faith, so as to remove mountains, but have not love, I am nothing. If I give away all I have, and if I deliver up my body to be burned, but have not love, I gain nothing.

> *Love is patient and kind; love does not envy or boast; it is not arrogant or rude. It does not insist on its own way; it is not irritable or resentful; it does not rejoice at wrongdoing, but rejoices with the truth. Love bears all things, believes all things, hopes all things, endures all things.*
>
> *Love never ends. As for prophecies, they will pass away; as for tongues, they will cease; as for knowledge, it will pass away. For we know in part and we prophesy in part, but when the perfect comes, the partial will pass away. When I was a child, I spoke like a child, I thought like a child, I reasoned like a child. When I became a man, I gave up childish ways. For now we see in a mirror dimly, but then face to face. Now I know in part; then I shall know fully, even as I have been fully known.*
>
> *So now faith, hope, and love abide, these three; but the greatest of these is love.* (1 Corinthians 13)

Paul knew that Jesus is not as interested in works like prophecy, casting out demons, and performing miracles as He is in acts of charity. He expects His disciples to proactively engage with those who are literally hungry and thirsty, or strangers and in prison, as well as those who are spiritually hungry and thirsty, or lost and unwittingly imprisoned by Satan.

Jesus also gave His disciples specific behavioral instructions during His last meal with them.

> *"A new commandment I give to you, that you love one another: just as I have loved you, you also are to love one another. By this all people will know that you are my disciples, if you have love for one another"* (John 13:34–35).

Though undoubtedly spoken in love, this is not merely a nice suggestion. It is a clear requisite characteristic for all who sincerely follow God. *"For this is the love of God, that we keep his commandments. And **his commandments are not burdensome**"* (1 John 5:3; emphasis added).

In an even broader application, Jesus spoke these words to the people during His Sermon on the Mount:

"You have heard that it was said, 'You shall love your neighbor and hate your enemy.' But I say to you, Love your enemies and pray for those who persecute you, so that you may be sons of your Father who is in heaven. For he makes his sun rise on the evil and on the good, and sends rain on the just and on the unjust. For if you love those who love you, what reward do you have? Do not even the tax collectors do the same? And if you greet only your brothers, what more are you doing than others? Do not even the Gentiles do the same? You therefore must be perfect, as your heavenly Father is perfect" (Matthew 5:43–48).

Living a loving and sacrificial life is the sign of true discipleship, even if it means we may suffer as Jesus indicated earlier in His discourse:

"Then they will deliver you up to tribulation and put you to death, and you will be hated by all nations for my name's sake. And then many will fall away and betray one another and hate one another. And many false prophets will arise and lead many astray. And because lawlessness will be increased, the love of many will grow cold. But the one who endures to the end will be saved" (Matthew 24:9–13).

Such faithfulness is not impossible. Jesus gave many comforting and encouraging promises to His disciples for strength in times of trouble. This one He shared with them before He was crucified.

"I have said these things to you, that in me you may have peace. In the world you will have tribulation. But take heart; ***I have overcome the world****"* (John 16:33; emphasis added).

If Jesus is continuing to address those who profess to follow Him through this message about the sheep and the goats—and within the context, there is no reason to believe otherwise—it would seem He is making one final and emphatic statement: it is not enough to simply profess or acknowledge His existence. We must also believe, just like Noah, and do everything Jesus asks. *"Whoever has my commandments and keeps them, he it is who loves me. And he who loves me will be loved by my father, and I will love him and manifest myself to him"* (John 14:21). Where does this love come from? *"We love because he first loved us"* (1 John 4:19).

For our sake [God] *made* [Jesus] *to be sin who knew no sin, so that in* [Jesus] *we might become the righteousness of God* (2 Corinthians 5:21).

God shows his love for us in that while we were still sinners, Christ died for us (Romans 5:8).

For God so loved the world, that he gave his only Son, that whoever believes in him should not perish but have eternal life. For God did not send his Son into the world to condemn the world, but in order that the world might be saved through him (John 3:16–17).

But when the goodness and loving kindness of God our Savior appeared, he saved us, not because of works done by us in righteousness, but according to his own mercy, by the washing of regeneration and renewal of the Holy Spirit, whom he poured out on us richly through Jesus Christ our Savior, so that being justified by his grace we might become heirs according to the hope of eternal life (Titus 3:4–7).

What is more significant than pinpointing which judgment Jesus is referring to is how He expects us to behave and live, remembering everyone that is in need both physically and spiritually.

Finally, consider the following passage from the book of Isaiah, where God addresses His people who feigned obedience through their fasting yet wondered why God was not answering their prayers:

"*Behold, you fast only to quarrel and to fight and to hit with a wicked fist. Fasting like yours this day will not make your voice to be heard on high. Is such the fast that I choose, a day for a person to humble himself? Is it to bow down his head like a reed, and to spread sackcloth and ashes under him? Will you call this a fast, and a day acceptable to the Lord? Is not this the fast that I choose: to loose the bonds of wickedness, to undo the straps of the yoke, to let the oppressed go free, and to break every yoke? Is it not to share your bread with the hungry and bring the homeless poor into your house; when you see the naked, to cover him, and not to hide yourself from your own flesh?* **Then shall your light break forth like the dawn, and your healing shall spring up speedily; your righteousness shall go before you; the glory of the Lord shall be your rear guard.** *Then you shall call, and the Lord will answer; you shall cry, and he will say, 'Here I am.' If you take away the yoke from your midst, the pointing of the finger, and speaking wickedness, if you pour yourself out for the hungry and satisfy the desire of the afflicted, then shall your light rise in the darkness and your gloom be as the noonday*" (Isaiah 58:4–10; emphasis added).

The story of the sheep and the goats concludes Jesus' Olivet Discourse. Further analogies could be made about the three stories contained in Matthew chapter 25, but certain key points are undeniable. Jesus expects His followers to know His Word accurately, follow Him closely, and be prepared for His return. He also expects us to care for His people in need. For those who do what Jesus asks, the rewards are beyond imagination; for those who do not, the warnings are ominous. Are you closely following Him or someone else, even yourself? God loved us enough to send His Son Jesus to show us the way.

"Everyone then who hears these words of mine and does them will be like a wise man who built his house on the rock. And the rain fell, and the floods came, and the winds blew and beat on that house, but it did not fall, because it had been founded on the rock. And everyone who hears these words of mine and does not do them will be like a foolish man who built his house on the sand. And the rain fell, and the floods came, and the winds blew and beat against that house, and it fell, and great was the fall of it" (Matthew 7:24–27).

There is just one thing remaining to complete our study of the Olivet Discourse. As Jesus was describing a key event that precedes His second coming, He said:

*"So when you see the **abomination of desolation** spoken of by the prophet Daniel, standing in the holy place (let the reader understand)…"* (Matthew 24:15; emphasis added).

Through the Olivet Discourse Jesus has given us a concise outline of the things that will take place both before and during the time of His return. But something essential is still missing in the greater picture: an actual timeline. To discover and unlock this next vital piece of information, Jesus points us to the book of Daniel.

And so our journey continues.

It is simply A Matter Of When

Chapter 10

The Seventy Weeks of Daniel, Part 1
(Daniel 9:1–26a)

Do You Know and Understand?

As it is with the Olivet Discourse, so it is with the book of Daniel. Interpretations are varied and scholars are divided. The controversies begin with whether or not it was even Daniel who wrote the book! Yeah, I know. In light of all this, how can we get a grip on what is right or wrong? In all actuality, there is no one alive who can completely and accurately interpret all end-time prophetic Scripture. But we are not meant to fully understand every detail. Jesus' instruction to His disciples is to *watch* and *pray* because much is still cloaked in mystery (Matthew 24:20, 25:13). We are given clues and signs to look for so that we will not be caught by surprise. If we stay alert, with a face value interpretation of Scripture, we can know enough about what is coming so that we will be prepared for Jesus' return (Matthew 24:43).

In His Olivet Discourse, Jesus' reference to the ***abomination of desolation*** in the book of Daniel is found in chapters 9 and 11. Yet aside from this, there is so much more to uncover in Daniel's writings about the end times. The book of Daniel is full of many specific details regarding what is to come as the end of our current world order unfolds. Utilizing a face value hermeneutic, I encourage you to dig into this amazing book for yourself.

Some things to consider as you do:

- Are the stories and visions Daniel recounts real?
- If they are real, what is their message?
- Does each sequential story or vision add additional perspective to help create a bigger picture about the *latter days*?
- What does the book of Daniel tell us about God's sovereignty and His control over world history?

Jesus knew that a considerable amount of what is written in the book of Daniel would help His disciples fill in the blanks from His Olivet Discourse. In fact, there is one particular section in Daniel that adds amazing clarity about end-time events that goes beyond a sequential outline. It contains the missing piece that specifies when the last years of current history will begin. For this we turn to Daniel chapter 9.

As we work through the various passages of Daniel chapter 9, remember the intent of this study. Although the analysis of the material presented here may initially seem logical enough, it is not meant to convince you of its accuracy. The challenge is for you to continue studying everything we are covering so that you come to your own well-researched understanding of these events. I simply caution you to beware of concluding that the latter days will be easy for the church. Jesus promised a *tribulation* that will be unlike anything the human race has ever experienced (Matthew

24:21). Always be prepared for the worst. Remember the parable of the ten virgins (Matthew 25:1–13).

We will not be covering Daniel's life other than to mention that as a young man of noble heritage he was taken captive by the Babylonians during the reign of Jehoiakim, king of Judah (607–597 BC). Along with some close friends, Daniel remained a part of the Babylonian and Medo-Persian courts throughout the rest of his life. The rest you will discover when you read the book of Daniel on your own.

Now let us focus on Daniel chapter 9.

In the first year of Darius the son of Ahasuerus, by descent a Mede, who was made king over the realm of the Chaldeans—in the first year of his reign, I, Daniel, perceived in the books the number of years that, according to the word of the LORD to Jeremiah the prophet, must pass before the end of the desolations of Jerusalem, namely, seventy years (verses 1–2).

As you can see, Daniel did some studying of his own. As he was reading through the writings of Jeremiah, the prophet Daniel came across this passage:

"Therefore thus says the Lord of hosts: Because you have not obeyed my words, behold, I will send for all the tribes of the north, declares the Lord, and for Nebuchadnezzar the king of Babylon, my servant, and I will bring them against this land and its inhabitants, and against all these surrounding nations. I will devote them to destruction, and make them a horror, a hissing, and an everlasting desolation. Moreover, I will banish from them the voice of mirth and the voice of gladness, the voice of the bridegroom and the voice of the bride, the grinding of the millstones and the light of the lamp. This whole land shall become a ruin and a waste, and these nations shall serve the king of Babylon seventy years. Then after seventy years are completed, I will punish the king

of Babylon and that nation, the land of the Chaldeans, for their iniquity, declares the Lord, making the land an everlasting waste. I will bring upon that land all the words that I have uttered against it, everything written in this book, which Jeremiah prophesied against all the nations. For many nations and great kings shall make slaves even of them, and I will recompense them according to their deeds and the work of their hands" (Jeremiah 25:8–14).

Daniel understood from the book of Jeremiah that the seventy-year captivity under the king of Babylon was almost over. The Babylonian exile began around 605 BC. Daniel wrote this passage shortly after the Babylonian Empire was overthrown by the Medes and Persians in 539 BC, or approximately four years before the completion of Jeremiah's seventy-year prophecy. Realizing this, Daniel begins to pray for his people:

Then I turned my face to the Lord God, seeking him by prayer and pleas for mercy with fasting and sackcloth and ashes. I prayed to the Lord *my God and made confession, saying, "O Lord, the great and awesome God, who keeps covenant and steadfast love with those who love him and keep his commandments, we have sinned and done wrong and acted wickedly and rebelled, turning aside from your commandments and rules. We have not listened to your servants the prophets, who spoke in your name to our kings, our princes, and our fathers, and to all the people of the land. To you, O Lord, belongs righteousness, but to us open shame, as at this day, to the men of Judah, to the inhabitants of Jerusalem, and to all Israel, those who are near and those who are far away, in all the lands to which you have driven them, because of the treachery that they have committed against you. To us, O Lord, belongs open shame, to our kings, to our princes, and to our fathers, because we have sinned against you. To the Lord our God belong mercy and forgiveness, for we have rebelled against him and have not obeyed the voice of the* L<small>ORD</small> *our God by walking in his laws, which he set before us by his servants the prophets. All Israel has transgressed your law and turned aside, refusing to obey your voice. And the curse and oath that are written in the Law of Moses the servant of God have been poured out upon us, because we have sinned against him"* (verses 3–11).

Daniel continues praying in the same manner, and then ends his supplication to God with the following:

"Now therefore, O our God, listen to the prayer of your servant and to his pleas for mercy, and for your own sake, O Lord, make your face to shine upon your sanctuary, which is desolate. O my God, incline your ear and hear. Open your eyes and see our desolations, and the city that is called by your name. For we do not present our pleas before you because of our righteousness, but because of your great mercy. O Lord, hear; O Lord, forgive. O Lord, pay attention and act. Delay not, for your own sake, O my God, because your city and your people are called by your name" (verses 17–19).

How appropriate for Jesus to refer His disciples to the writings of Daniel. They contain a treasure trove of additional information about end-time events. Aside from this, Daniel's reference to the book of Jeremiah is sobering. There are many striking parallels between the sins of the nation of Israel in Jeremiah's day and the picture Jesus paints of many claiming to follow Him as His second coming nears. We would all do well to pray like Daniel for the church, our nation, and ourselves.

Knowing that the destruction of Jerusalem and the exile of the nation of Israel from the land of Canaan—the Promised Land—was the direct result of their continual disobedience, which God warned them of through Moses,

Daniel was praying for God to fulfill another promise He gave to Moses.

"And when all these things come upon you, the blessing and the curse, which I have set before you, and you call them to mind among all the nations where the Lord your God has driven you, and return to the Lord your God, you and your children, and obey his voice in all that I command you today, with all your heart and with all your soul, then the Lord your God will restore your fortunes and have mercy on you, and he will gather you again from all the peoples where the Lord your God has scattered you. And the Lord your God will bring you into the land that your fathers possessed, that you may possess it. And he will make you more prosperous and numerous than your fathers" (Deuteronomy 30:1–3, 5).

Daniel's plea was for forgiveness and mercy as the completion of the seventy-year exile drew near. But God planned something even more magnificent that would far transcend simply answering Daniel's prayers. God wanted to reveal to Daniel another time of *seventy*, a vision of tremendous magnitude about extraordinary things yet to come that would bring an end to sin forever. (For the remainder of verses quoted from Daniel chapter 9 through Daniel chapter 12, we will use the New International Version [NIV] unless otherwise stated. All other passages quoted are taken from the ESV.)

While I was speaking and praying, confessing my sin and the sin of my people Israel and making my request to the Lord my God for his holy hill—while I was still in prayer, Gabriel, the man I had seen in the earlier vision, came to me in swift flight about the time of the evening sacrifice. He instructed me and said to me, "Daniel, I have now come to give you insight and understanding. As soon as you began to pray, a word went out, which I have come to tell you, for you are highly esteemed. Therefore, consider the word and understand the vision: Seventy **'sevens'** [or seventy **weeks**; ESV, NASB, KJV] *are decreed for your people and your holy city to finish transgression, to put an end to sin, to atone for wickedness, to bring in everlasting righteousness, to seal up vision and prophecy and to anoint the Most Holy Place"* (verses 20–24; emphasis added).

The *earlier vision* referred to by Daniel is recorded in chapter 8:15–17 when *one having the appearance of a man* sent the angel Gabriel (Luke 1:19, 26; all of Daniel 8) to help Daniel understand a vision he had just received. Here again, Gabriel appears to Daniel. This time Gabriel tells Daniel he is *highly esteemed* by God and that his prayers have been heard. And so the vision begins:

"Seventy 'sevens' are decreed for your people and your holy city." According to Gabriel, these *seventy sevens* will:

- *Finish transgression.*
- *Put an end to sin.*
- *Atone for wickedness.*
- *Bring in everlasting righteousness.*
- *Seal up vision and prophecy.*
- *Anoint the Most Holy Place.*

Many of the controversies surrounding Daniel chapter 9 hinge on whether or not all the points listed above from Daniel's vision have already taken place. Then there is the "literal versus symbolic" debate. However, there is absolutely nothing in the context of the message indicating that we should accept its details other than literally. This is why the initial part of our study focused on mindset and method of interpretation. We cannot approach God's Word with a personal agenda, or desired outcome, without sacrificing God's intended message. A heart and mind free of personal filters, combined with a face value hermeneutic, will give us our best chance of interpreting Scripture correctly.

It is important to note that many of the prophetic messages God gave Daniel were fulfilled in his lifetime, while others were not. Some of the visions Daniel received were actually beyond his understanding. Toward the end of his final vision, covered in Daniel chapters 10–12, Daniel was told:

"But you, Daniel shut up the words and seal the book, until the time of the end." I heard, but I did not understand. Then I said, "O my lord, what shall be the outcome of these things?" He said, "Go your way, Daniel, for the words are shut up and sealed until the time of the end" (Daniel 12:4a, 8–9).

The clarity we need to correctly interpret some prophecies will only come with time.

Continuing with Daniel chapter 9:

"Know and understand this: From the time the word goes out to restore and rebuild Jerusalem until the Anointed One, the ruler, comes, there will be seven 'sevens,' and sixty-two 'sevens.' It will be rebuilt with streets and a trench, but in times of trouble. After the sixty-two 'sevens,' the Anointed One will be put to death and will have nothing. The people of the ruler who will come will destroy the city and the sanctuary. The end will come like a flood: War will continue until the end, and desolations have been decreed. He will confirm a covenant with many for one 'seven.' In the middle of the 'seven' he will put an end to sacrifice and offering. And at the temple he will set up an abomination that causes desolation, until the end that is decreed is poured out on him" (verses 25–27).

Let us break this message down in raw terms:

- We can easily assume that *seventy sevens* (or *seventy weeks*) is a measurement of time. Exactly how much time is not immediately clear.

- The message states that there will be a specific moment when *the word goes out to restore and rebuild Jerusalem*. This is fairly easy to pin down.
- From this decree *to restore and rebuild Jerusalem* until the coming of *the Anointed One*, there are apparently *seven sevens* and *sixty-two sevens*, for a total of sixty-nine *sevens*.
- It would appear from the text that there is a reason for the separation of the *seven sevens* and the *sixty-two sevens*. Since it states that *"after the sixty-two sevens … the Anointed One will be put to death and have nothing,"* it is quite possible that the *seven sevens* is directly related to the rebuilding of Jerusalem *with streets and a trench, but in times of trouble*.
- There could arise a question as to whether or not the *seven sevens* and *sixty-two sevens* begin at the same time. But when analyzing the entire text, it becomes obvious that they are separate. *Seven* plus *sixty-two* plus *one* equals *seventy*. If the *seven* and *sixty-two* were to begin at the same time, the total would only be sixty-three *sevens* instead of *seventy*. Therefore, according to the text, the order of *sevens* comes in units of *seven*, *sixty-two*, and *one* for a total of *seventy sevens*.
- With the prior point in mind, it would seem that *the Anointed One will be put to death and have nothing* at sixty-nine *sevens*, which will be after *the word* [goes out] *to restore and rebuild Jerusalem*.
- Then there is the question of *the people of the ruler who will come* [who] *will destroy the city and the sanctuary*. In context, this is presumably about Jerusalem and the temple. But who is the ruler? Does this happen during the remaining one *seven*?

- Also, who is the *he* that *will confirm a covenant with many for one seven* [and] *in the middle of the seven put an end to sacrifice and offering* [and] *set up an **abomination that causes desolation***? Is this *he* the same ruler *who will come* [and] *destroy the city and the sanctuary*? Is this also part of the remaining one *seven*?
- Finally, does the remaining one *seven* directly follow the other sixty-nine or is it somehow separate?

Unlike the other messages given to Daniel, there is no further information provided as to its meaning. Would Daniel have understood any part of the vision without more clarification? Daniel might have speculated that the *seventy sevens* were actually *seventy weeks* of seven years. In Strong's Concordance, the Hebrew word *shabua* has been translated both *seven* and *week* as it literally means a period of seven. But aside from this, Daniel would have perceived little more. We, however, have the distinct advantage of history on our side. As we put together the historical timeline concerning *"the word ... to restore and rebuild Jerusalem"* and when *"the Anointed One will be put to death and have nothing,"* we can map out the fulfillment of sixty-nine of the *seventy sevens*, confirming that they are indeed *seventy* weeks of seven years. Then there is only one *week* of seven years left—the final *seven* of the *seventy*—to consider.

In order to accurately understand the math from Daniel's vision, we cannot follow our modern-day Gregorian solar calendar that is based on the revolution of Earth around the sun. The prophetic calendar of the Bible is lunar-based and is determined by the moon's revolution around Earth. It comprises 12 months of 30 days, or a 360-day year. Using Scripture to interpret Scripture, we find one example of this in Revelation 11:

"... for it is given over to the nations, and they will trample the holy city for forty-two months. And I will grant

authority to my two witnesses, and they will prophesy for 1,260 days, clothed in sackcloth" (Revelation 11:2b–3).

In this example, there is an implied correlation of the *forty-two months* with *1,260 days* or three and a half lunar-based years. Another example is found in Revelation 12:

"… and the woman fled into the wilderness, where she has a place prepared by God, in which she is to be nourished for 1,260 days. But the woman was given the two wings of a great eagle so that she might fly from the serpent into the wilderness, to the place where she is to be nourished for a time, and times, and half a time" (Revelation 12:6, 14).

Here again we see that *1,260 days* is associated with *a time, and times, and half a time,* or three and a half lunar calendar years. It is interesting to note that Daniel used similar language in chapter 7 of his writings:

He shall speak words against the Most High, and shall wear out the saints of the Most High, and shall think to change the times and the law; and they shall be given into his hand for a time, times, and half a time (Daniel 7:25).

As mentioned before, the enemy of our souls, Satan, is alive and well—so far—and is relentless in his mission to do whatever he can to confuse God's children with every means possible, including changing calendars. Nevertheless, with a face value hermeneutic, and allowing Scripture to interpret Scripture, we can uncover hidden mysteries that bring us closer to understanding God's intended message.

THE MATH

There are two things we must do in order to accurately calculate the period of the sixty-nine weeks that begin at *"the time the word goes out to restore and rebuild Jerusalem"* and end when *"the Anointed One* [is] *put to death and will have nothing"* (verses 25a, 26a).

1) Determine the actual date that the *word* [went] *out to restore and rebuild Jerusalem.*
2) Reconcile the biblical prophetic lunar calendar with our current Gregorian solar calendar by which BC dates have been derived.

There are different dates attributed to when the word was given to *restore and rebuild Jerusalem.* One of these is 538 BC, when Cyrus gave the Jews permission to rebuild the temple in Jerusalem.

Now in the first year of Cyrus king of Persia, that the word of the Lord by the mouth of Jeremiah might be fulfilled, the Lord stirred up the spirit of Cyrus king of Persia, so that he made a proclamation throughout all his kingdom and also put it in writing: "Thus says Cyrus king of Persia, 'The LORD, the God of heaven, has given me all the kingdoms of the earth, and he has charged me to build him a house at Jerusalem, which is in Judah. Whoever is among you of all his people, may the LORD his God be with him. Let him go up'" (2 Chronicles 36:22–23).

However, this proclamation by Cyrus mentions nothing about rebuilding the city of Jerusalem, only the temple. Permission to begin rebuilding the city came from Artaxerxes during the time of Nehemiah. This occurred around March or April of 444 BC. Nehemiah writes:

In the month of Nisan, in the twentieth year of King Artaxerxes, when wine was before him, I took up the wine and gave it to the king. Now I had not been sad in his presence. And the king said to me, "Why is your face sad, seeing you are not sick? This is nothing but sadness of the heart." Then I was very much afraid. I said to the king, "Let the king live forever! Why should not my face be sad, when the city, the place of my fathers' graves, lies in ruins, and its gates have been destroyed by fire?" Then the king said to me, "What are you requesting?" So I prayed to the God of heaven. And I said to the king, "If it pleases the king, and if your servant has found favor in your sight, that you send me to Judah, to the city of my fathers' graves, that I may rebuild it." And the king said to me (the queen sitting beside him), "How long will you be gone, and when will you return?" So it pleased the king to send me when I had given him a time. And I said to the king, "If it pleases the king, let letters be given me to the governors of the province Beyond the River, that they may let me pass through until I come to Judah, and a letter to Asaph, the keeper of the king's forest, that he may give me timber to make beams for the gates of the fortress of the temple, and for the wall of the city, and for the house that I shall occupy." And the king granted me what I asked, for the good hand of my God was upon me (Nehemiah 2:1–8).

The *times of trouble* Nehemiah experienced while rebuilding, as mentioned to Daniel in verse 25, are detailed in the book of Nehemiah, chapters 2–7. In total, the reconstruction took approximately 49 years, or *seven weeks* of *seven* years, thus fulfilling the first unit of the *seventy sevens* message given to Daniel.

Now that we have an approximate date of 444 BC for when the restoration and rebuilding of Jerusalem began, we must reconcile the biblical calendar with our current Gregorian calendar. To do this, we first convert the sixty-nine *sevens* into the actual number of days according to the biblical lunar calendar:

- Sixty-nine *sevens* or 69 × 7 = 483 total lunar calendar years in Daniel's vision.
- 483 years × 360 days per year in the biblical lunar calendar = 173,880 lunar calendar days.

It is simply A Matter Of When

- Our Gregorian calendar year equals 365.242 days.
- Dividing the number of biblical lunar calendar days by the number of days per year in our current Gregorian calendar, we get the number of years in Daniel's message according to our current Gregorian calendar: 173,880 biblical lunar calendar days in Daniel's vision ÷ 365.242 days per year in our current Gregorian calendar = 476.07 equivalent years for Daniel's vision using today's Gregorian calendar.

Taking the equivalent Gregorian calendar sixty-nine *sevens* of years (476), and subtracting the starting date *to restore and rebuild Jerusalem* (444 BC), we get AD 32. But since there is no "0" AD, as the years went directly from 1 BC to AD 1, the actual result is AD 33 when *the Anointed One will be put to death and will have nothing* (verse 26a).

We can crunch the numbers and dates however we wish, but it is no coincidence that the crucifixion of Jesus was right around this time. If there is any apparent error in math concerning the date *to restore and rebuild Jerusalem* and the *Anointed One* [being] *put to death and* [having] *nothing*, it is not the fault of the message given to Daniel but comes from the confusion with modified calendars. Satan is the author of confusion, and his plan is to keep God's children from the truth. Does this seem too complicated or too simple? You decide. Do your research. Access to information is unprecedented today. I only caution you to look carefully. Be like the Jews at Berea (Acts 17:11).

Is the controversy over? Hardly. We still must deal with *the prince who is to come* and the one *seven* or seven years left of the *seventy sevens* from God's message to Daniel. Has this remaining *seven* already passed or is there something yet to be fulfilled? For those who will be alive when Jesus returns, the answer to this question may just be the most important part of the message.

Chapter 11

The Seventy Weeks of Daniel, Part 2
(Daniel 9:26b–27)

Are You Ready for the "Ruler" and the Final Week of Current World History?

In the previous chapter we outlined what the *seventy sevens* message to Daniel (Daniel 9:24) is supposed to accomplish:

- *Finish transgression.*
- *Put an end to sin.*
- *Atone for wickedness.*
- *Bring in everlasting righteousness.*
- *Seal up vision and prophecy.*
- *Anoint the Most Holy Place.*

So far in our study of Daniel chapter 9, we have determined the approximate dates *to restore and rebuild Jerusalem* and when *the Anointed One will be put to death and will have nothing.* It was circa 444 BC when Artaxerxes gave Nehemiah permission to return to Jerusalem and rebuild the city. Nehemiah spent *seven sevens*, or roughly 49 years, on this project *in times of trouble* (Nehemiah chapters 2–7, Daniel 9:25). Around AD 33 the *Anointed One*, Jesus, was crucified *sixty-two sevens* or 434 years after Nehemiah's work was completed (Daniel 9:25–26a; see **Chapter 10** for full analysis). This literally fulfills sixty-nine of the *seventy sevens*. There is only one *seven*, or seven-year period, remaining in Daniel's vision to accomplish all six points above.

This leaves us with two important questions:

1. Which of the points listed above from Daniel 9:24 were fulfilled at the completion of the sixty-nine *sevens* that culminated at the time of Jesus' death?
2. What is the timeframe of the last *seven*, or seven-year period, of Daniel's vision, and how does it play into the remainder of the message? (Daniel 9:26b–27)

Let us start with the first question.

Continuing with our face value hermeneutic, the one point on the list above that we should be able to check off is *atone for wickedness*. The death of Jesus on the cross was the ultimate sacrifice required for reconciliation with God.

But now in Christ Jesus you who once were far off have been brought near by the blood of Christ. For he himself is our peace, who has made us both one and has broken down in his flesh the dividing wall of hostility by abolishing the law of commandments expressed in ordinances, that he might create in himself one new man in place of the two, so making peace, and might reconcile us both to God in one body through the cross, thereby killing the hostility. And he came and preached peace to you who were far off and peace to those who were near. For through him we both have access in one Spirit to the Father (Ephesians 2:13–18).

For in him all the fullness of God was pleased to dwell, and through him to reconcile to himself all things, whether on earth or in heaven, making peace by the blood of his cross (Colossians 1:19–20).

Therefore, if anyone is in Christ, he is a new creation. The old has passed away; behold, the new has come. All this is from God, who through Christ reconciled us to himself and gave us the ministry of reconciliation; that is, in Christ God was reconciling the world to himself, not counting their trespasses against them, and entrusting to us the message of reconciliation (2 Corinthians 5:17–19).

For the judgment following one trespass [in the Garden of Eden] *brought condemnation, but the free gift following many trespasses brought justification. For if, because of one man's* [Adam's] *trespass, death reigned through that one man, much more will those who receive the abundance of grace and the free gift of righteousness reign in life through the one man Jesus Christ. Therefore, as one trespass led to condemnation for all men, so one act of righteousness* [Jesus' unmerited sacrifice on the cross for our sins] *leads to justification and life for all men. For as by the one man's* [Adam's] *disobedience the many were made sinners, so by the one man's* [Jesus'] *obedience the many will be made righteous* (Romans 5:16b–19).

As for all the other points on the list derived from Daniel 9:24 of what the *seventy sevens* are said to accomplish, interpretations concerning their fulfillment are numerous. Some argue that Jesus' death and resurrection accomplished all of them either literally, symbolically, or spiritually. In light of the fact that the rebuilding of Jerusalem and the death of *the Anointed One* were actual events that completed sixty-nine of the *seventy sevens*, there is no sound basis for expecting anything other than a literal fulfillment for the last and final *week*. So what about the remaining points from Daniel 9:24? Have they literally been fulfilled?

Let us examine this further.

Who is the intended audience of this message? The angel Gabriel affirms that the vision concerns Daniel's people, the physical Children of Israel (verse 24). Although those that believe in Jesus *have been set free from sin* (Romans 6:22), the rest of the world has not. This includes anyone, including the Children of Israel, who has not accepted Jesus as the Messiah.

Jesus warns that sin and lawlessness will increase as His second coming nears.

"Then they will deliver you [all of Jesus' true followers] *up to tribulation and put you to death, and you will be hated by all nations for my name's sake. And then many will fall away and betray one another and hate one another. And many false prophets will arise and lead many astray. And because lawlessness will be increased, the love of many will grow cold"* (Matthew 24:9–12).

Can we honestly say that the other five points from Daniel 9:24 have been literally fulfilled? Transgression and sin are not eradicated from the world. Jerusalem is in a constant state of turmoil. Righteousness is "relative" in our society and far from the righteousness that God desires. Based on what Jesus told His disciples in the Olivet Discourse about the ever-increasing calamities that will envelop the world as His return nears, it would seem all the remaining points on the list—

- *Finish transgression.*
- *Put an end to sin.*
- *Bring in everlasting righteousness.*
- *Seal up vision and prophecy.*
- *Anoint the Most Holy Place.*

—can only be fulfilled once Jesus literally returns.

Before we tackle the second question above regarding the timeframe of the final seven-year period of Daniel's vision, let us take a look at the remaining verses from the message Gabriel gave to Daniel.

"*The people of the ruler who will come will destroy the city and the sanctuary. The end will come like a flood: War will continue until the end, and desolations have been decreed. He will confirm a covenant with many for one 'seven.' In the middle of the 'seven' he will put an end to sacrifice and offering. And at the temple he will set up an **abomination that causes desolation**, until the end that is decreed is poured out on him*" (Daniel 9:26b–27; emphasis added).

In light of these verses, let us consider the following for question two above:

- We are studying Daniel chapter 9 because in His Olivet Discourse Jesus references the **abomination of desolation** (Matthew 24:15), an event that is mentioned in this chapter of the book of Daniel.
- According to Jesus, the **abomination of desolation** is placed in the temple at Jerusalem directly preceding the **great tribulation**, which itself is immediately followed by His return.
- The correlation of the **abomination of desolation** and Jesus' return would seem to place this part of Daniel's *seventy sevens* vision at or around the time of the end.
- With sixty-nine *sevens* fulfilled following the death of Jesus, it would seem that the rest of Gabriel's message to Daniel, as recounted in chapter 9:26b–27, will transpire during the remaining one *seven* of seven years.
- Is Jesus indicating to His disciples that this final seven-year period of Daniel's *seventy sevens* vision will come at the end of our world as we know it? According

to a face value interpretation of Scripture, and what Gabriel tells Daniel that the *seventy sevens* will accomplish (Daniel 9:24), this would appear to be the case.

Jesus seems to be giving those of His disciples living near the time of His return an important key to help them unlock the mystery of this remaining seven-year period from Daniel 9:27. Every prophecy, in both Matthew 24 and Daniel 9, that has already come to pass was fulfilled literally. Aside from the Messiah being *cut off* with His death on a cross, examples include the invasion of Jerusalem by Titus in AD 70 that fulfilled Daniel 9:26a as well as the continually increasing world tensions and natural disasters mentioned in Matthew 24:6–8. Therefore, are the remaining prophecies mentioned in both His Olivet Discourse and Daniel's *seventy sevens* vision also destined to come to pass literally and within this remaining seven-year timespan?

Let us examine the events that are yet to take place from Daniel's *seventy sevens* vision as recounted in Daniel 9:26b–27.

- *The people of the ruler who will come will destroy the city and the sanctuary.*
- *The end will come like a flood: War will continue until the end, and desolations have been decreed.*
- *He will confirm a covenant with many for one 'seven.'*
- *In the middle of the 'seven' he will put an end to sacrifice and offering. And at the temple he will set up an **abomination that causes desolation**, until the end that is decreed is poured out on him.*

Here is what we should be able to assume using a face value hermeneutic:

- In His Olivet Discourse, Jesus places the ***abomination of desolation*** mentioned in the writings of Daniel during the time of His return.
- With all the other aforementioned events from the Olivet Discourse and Daniel 9 having been literally fulfilled, we should likewise assume that this ***abomination of desolation*** event Jesus is referring to will literally take place very close to His return.
- Based on the sequence of events Jesus carefully outlines in His Olivet Discourse, we know that Jesus has not yet returned. (Refer to earlier chapters of this book for a detailed analysis.)
- With only one period of seven years remaining in Daniel's *seventy sevens* vision, and the other sixty-nine *sevens* completed with the death of Jesus, we can assume that the remaining events from Daniel 9:26b–27 and the Olivet Discourse (Matthew 24:15–31) will all be literally fulfilled during this final seven-year period at the time of Jesus' return.

We know from history that there have been various invasions of Jerusalem along with desecrations of its temple. (See earlier discussions about Antiochus IV Epiphanes and Titus in **Chapter 5**.) However, none of these were followed by Jesus' literal return as outlined in His discourse.

Based on the analysis above, which do you think is easier?

1. Accept a literal interpretation of the events in the Olivet Discourse and Daniel's *seventy sevens* vision, including the interconnection Jesus gives them concerning His return to Earth,

OR

2. Accept the idea that the remaining points from both the Olivet Discourse and Daniel chapter 9 have already been fulfilled either symbolically or spiritually?

It is Simply A Matter Of When

What do you think? What does Scripture say? Knowing how much has already been literally fulfilled in the Scriptures we are studying, is there any reason we should doubt that the rest should follow the same pattern? There is absolutely nothing in the context that would suggest otherwise.

For the sake of consistency in our face value study of the Olivet Discourse, let us take another look at Daniel 9:26b–27 in the same light to see what we can surmise at this point:

- What remains of Daniel's *seventy sevens* vision should all come to pass within a period of seven biblical lunar calendar years of 360 days each as explained in **Chapter 10**.
- It would seem that *He* [who] *will confirm a covenant with many* for seven years is the same as the *ruler* whose people *will destroy the city and the sanctuary*. There are no indicators implying differently.
- *The end will come like a flood: War will continue until the end, and desolations have been decreed*. Does this sound reminiscent of many things Jesus mentions in His Olivet Discourse?
- Halfway through this seven years, or midway into the *covenant*, this ruler *will put an end to sacrifice and offering. And at the temple he will set up an **abomination that causes desolation**, until the end that is decreed is poured out on him*.
- According to the Olivet Discourse, this **abomination of desolation** initiates the **great tribulation**, which is immediately followed by Jesus' return. In other words, by correlating the **abomination of desolation** with His return, Jesus places this event in the book of Daniel—along with the rest of His discourse—at the *time of the end*.

What we do not yet know:

- The date this final seven-year period begins.
- Who this *ruler* actually is.
- Exactly what the confirmed *covenant with many* will entail.
- What the ***abomination of desolation*** is specifically.

What we do know:

- The final seven years of the *seventy sevens* vision Gabriel gave to Daniel begins with a *covenant* between this *ruler* and *many.*
- In the middle of these seven years, or three and a half years after the *covenant* is confirmed, the *ruler* eliminates temple sacrifice and sets up *an **abomination that causes desolation** until the end that is decreed is poured out on him.*

Does all this seem complicated? Do not let it be. We may not have all the answers yet, but Jesus is giving us enough information so that we should know how to *watch*, and what to watch for, as the end draws near (Matthew 24:42–43, 25:13).

What we should be looking for:

- A *ruler* to arise that makes an important *covenant with many.* There is speculation that this *ruler* is the final antichrist, the one the apostle Paul calls *"the man of lawlessness … the son of destruction, who opposes and exalts himself against every so-called god or object of worship, so that he takes his seat in the temple of God, proclaiming himself to be God"* (2 Thessalonians 2:1–

12). The *covenant with many* might be a pact that the *ruler* makes with Israel and its neighbors that brings about some sort of temporary peace in the Mideast. An event like this would be quite newsworthy.

- The vision further states, *"In the middle of the 'seven'* [the ruler] *will put an end to sacrifice and offering. And at the temple he will set up an **abomination that causes desolation**."* There is much speculation surrounding this passage, as there are many unanswered questions concerning how this part of Daniel's vision might unfold. For example, to *put an end to sacrifice and offering* and to *set up an* **abomination that causes desolation** in the temple at Jerusalem, there would seemingly need to be a Jewish temple in Jerusalem—and currently there is not. Discussions as to exactly how this could take place range from where the Temple Mount is actually located to secret preparations being made to rebuild it. (I encourage you to do your own research on this issue.) But once these events take shape, in whatever literal form they become manifest, the vision indicates that there will be only three and a half years left before all the points outlined in Daniel 9:24 are fulfilled. According to the Olivet Discourse, this is also when Jesus returns and judgment begins.

What can we take away from Daniel's *seventy sevens* vision given him by the angel Gabriel?

- If we are watching closely enough, we should be able to recognize the signing of, or an agreement to, a major *covenant* that may involve the Middle East and is confirmed by some emerging *ruler.*
- According to Daniel's *seventy sevens* vision, only three and a half years will pass until this *ruler* breaks the *covenant*

and sets up his ***abomination that causes desolation*** in the temple. And according to the Olivet Discourse, this event is the precursor to the ***great tribulation***, which is immediately followed by Jesus' return.
- Finally, this *ruler* that sets up the ***abomination that causes desolation*** will continue *until the end that is decreed is poured out on him*. The apostle Paul says, "*the Lord Jesus will kill* [the lawless one] *with the breath of his mouth and bring to nothing by the appearance of his coming*" (2 Thessalonians 2:8). When Jesus returns, this lawless ruler will surely meet his end.

In summary, here is what it seems we should understand, so far, based on Jesus' connecting the ***abomination that causes desolation*** in the book of Daniel with His Olivet Discourse in Matthew chapter 24:

- The *covenant* that is apparently confirmed by this *ruler* will initiate the beginning of the remaining one *seven* of seven years in Daniel's *seventy sevens* vision.
- From here, the clock starts ticking. At this point there is literally only seven years left of current world history and the completion of all that remains to be fulfilled from Daniel's vision (Daniel 9:24).
- Since this *ruler* breaks the *covenant* and [sets] *up an **abomination that causes desolation*** halfway into this final seven-year period, it means we will only have the first three and a half years of this final seven-year period to prepare before the ***great tribulation*** befalls Earth.

From an outline of events in the Olivet Discourse to an actual timeline in Daniel chapter 9, it seems we have an adequate picture of what is to come and what to watch for.

The Olivet Discourse gives us the sequence; Daniel chapter 9 pinpoints the final countdown. Will you be ready? It is simply a matter of when.

Some might argue, "But why prepare? What difference will it make? If it is meant to happen, then let it happen!" But according to Jesus, it matters tremendously, and He gives us some very specific instructions to guide us through it all.

*"So when you see the **abomination of desolation** spoken of by the prophet Daniel, standing in the holy place (**let the reader understand**), then let those who are in Judea flee to the mountains. Let the one who is on the housetop not go down to take what is in his house, and let the one who is in the field not turn back to take his cloak. And alas for women who are pregnant and for those who are nursing infants in those days! Pray that your flight may not be in winter or on a Sabbath. For then there will be **great tribulation**, such as has not been from the beginning of the world until now, no, and never will be"* (Matthew 24:15–21; emphasis added).

Once this final *abomination* is set in place, as foretold by Jesus in the Olivet Discourse, time will be running out. The **great tribulation** will be upon us. We have the luxury of Jesus' preemptive warning if we are actively watching as He suggests. Between the confirming of the *covenant* and the **abomination of desolation** being set up, we will each have approximately three and a half years to decide what to do and prepare accordingly. Based on what Jesus told His disciples, it would seem that many of us, if not most, should be getting out of town and heading toward the mountains or similar isolated areas. Some might feel called to stay behind to warn others of all that is coming in the hopes that a few might hear, receive the truth, and be saved.

Those that can determine who this *ruler* is, and can recognize the *covenant* he *confirms*, should have this ample time of three and a half years to prepare. There is a lot at stake, not only for us, but also for our family, friends, and loved ones.

Should we take Jesus at His word literally and at face value? Is there any reason why you think we should not?

There is one more reference to the ***abomination of desolation*** in Daniel's writings. It is found in chapter 11 of his book.

Let us take a brief look.

It is simply A Matter Of When

Chapter 12

The Final Vision of Daniel
(Daniel chapters 10–12)

Those Who Are Wise Shall Understand

This remarkable vision given to Daniel outlines with amazing detail many of the world's conflicts from the time of Daniel (during the 6th and 5th centuries BC) to the end of our current world order. It is so accurate that some believe Daniel wrote at least the initial part after the conflicts described had already taken place. However, this would make Daniel somewhat of a fraud. And since Daniel was not around when Christ died, yet he accurately pinpointed the time of His death (see previous study on Daniel chapter 9), there should not be any surprises here. *"For the testimony of Jesus is the spirit of prophecy"* (Revelation 19:10). Fulfilled prophecy is meant to increase our faith in prophecies that are yet unfulfilled, that they will also come to pass exactly as God gave them.

Our overview of Daniel's final vision, contained in Daniel chapters 10 through 12, will be brief. The majority of our study has already been completed with the discussion of the Olivet Discourse and Daniel chapter 9. However, the **abomination of desolation** that Jesus talks about in His discourse is also mentioned in Daniel chapter 11, verse 31. Therefore, in following Jesus' admonition to *let the reader understand* (Matthew 24:15), we will consider some important additional information given to Daniel by *the man clothed in linen* (Daniel 10:5, 12:6–7).

Daniel chapter 10 introduces Daniel's final vision and is something you can enjoy reading on your own. We will not be covering most of the prophesied conflicts recounted in the first part of Daniel chapter 11 because they do not directly pertain to our study. (The ESV Study Bible has some valuable commentary on this.)

History shows that a significant portion of Daniel's vision in chapter 11 has already come to pass. Later in the chapter, however, a shift in focus is made to *the time of the end* that runs through chapter 12. As we discussed earlier in the near/far implication and application of some biblical prophecies (see **Chapter 2**), certain information in these passages can pertain both to a near fulfillment and a future, or ultimate, fulfillment.

Many scholars believe that Antiochus IV Epiphanes is the ruler described in Daniel 11 beginning with verse 21. This section of the vision certainly seems to have accurately predicted many of his movements and actions. Antiochus was undoubtedly a type of antichrist, a ruler who wreaked havoc in Jerusalem and horribly desecrated the Jewish temple. But Antiochus' reign of terror did not directly precede the *time of the end* as is indicated to Daniel in the message. So although this part of Daniel's final vision may be a reference to Antiochus IV Epiphanes in a near sense, an ultimate fulfillment by the final antichrist is still to come.

Starting with Daniel 11:21, we will begin to see some words or phrases that are similar to those used in Daniel's *seventy sevens* vision from Daniel chapter 9.

"He will be succeeded by a contemptible person who has not been given the honor of royalty. He will invade the kingdom when its people feel secure, and he will seize it through intrigue. Then an overwhelming army will be swept away before him; both it and a prince of the covenant will be destroyed. After coming to an agreement with him, he will act deceitfully, and with only a few people he will rise to power. When the richest provinces feel secure, he will invade them and will achieve what neither his fathers nor his forefathers did. He will distribute plunder, loot and wealth among his followers. He will plot the overthrow of fortresses—but only for a time.

"With a large army he will stir up his strength and courage against the king of the South. The king of the South will wage war with a large and very powerful army, but he will not be able to stand because of the plots devised against him. Those who eat from the king's provisions will try to destroy him; his army will be swept away, and many will fall in battle. The two kings, with their hearts bent on evil, will sit at the same table and lie to each other, but to no avail, because an end will still come at the appointed time. The king of the North will return to his own country with great wealth, but his heart will be set against the holy covenant. He will take action against it and then return to his own country.

"At the appointed time he will invade the South again, but this time the outcome will be different from what it was before. Ships of the western coastlands will oppose him, and he will lose heart. Then he will turn back and vent his fury against the holy covenant. He will return and show favor to those who forsake the holy covenant.

"His armed forces will rise up to desecrate the temple fortress and will abolish the daily sacrifice. Then they will set up the **abomination that causes desolation**. With flattery he will corrupt those who have violated the covenant, but the people who know their God will firmly resist him.

"Those who are wise will instruct many, though for a time they will fall by the sword or be burned or captured or plundered. When they fall, they will receive a little help, and many who are not sincere will join them. Some of the wise will stumble, so that they may be refined, purified and made spotless until the time of the end, for it will still come at the appointed time.

"The king will do as he pleases. He will exalt and magnify himself above every god and will say unheard-of things against the God of gods. He will be successful until the time of wrath is completed, for what has been determined must take place. He will show no regard for the gods of his ancestors or for the one desired by women, nor will he regard any god, but will exalt himself above them all. Instead of them, he will honor a god of fortresses; a god unknown to his ancestors he will honor with gold and silver, with precious stones and costly gifts. He will attack the mightiest fortresses with the help of a foreign god and will greatly honor those who acknowledge him. He will make them rulers over many people and will distribute the land at a price.

"At the time of the end the king of the South will engage him in battle, and the king of the North will storm out against him with chariots and cavalry and a great fleet of ships. He will invade many countries and sweep through them like a flood. He will also invade the Beautiful Land. Many countries will fall, but Edom, Moab and the leaders of Ammon will be delivered from his hand. He will extend his power over many countries; Egypt will not escape. He *will gain control of the treasures of gold and silver and all the riches of Egypt, with the Libyans and Cushites in submission. But reports from the east and the north will alarm him, and he will set out in a great rage to destroy and annihilate many. He will pitch his royal tents between the seas at the beautiful holy mountain. Yet he will come to his end, and no one will help him."* (Daniel 11:21–45; emphasis added)

As it was with the *seventy sevens* vision of Daniel, a heavenly messenger tells Daniel of an important covenant, an end to daily sacrifice, desecration of the temple, and the placing of an ***abomination that causes desolation.*** Although there are many similarities to the conflicts and actions of Antiochus IV Epiphanes in this section of Scripture, there are also some strong indications that Daniel's vision is about something that is yet to happen *"at the time of the end"* (Daniel 11:40).

Let us consider a few of them.

"The king will do as he pleases" (verse 36a).

This was only partially true about Antiochus, a Greek Seleucid king. By the time of Antiochus' reign (175–164 BC), the Romans had become considerably more powerful than the Greeks. At one point during Antiochus' second attack on Egypt in 168 BC, an old Roman ambassador, Gaius Popillius Laenas, drew a line in the sand around Antiochus. Gaius demanded that before Antiochus stepped one foot across the line he needed to decide to either abandon Egypt or face war with Rome. Antiochus agreed to leave.

"He will exalt and magnify himself above every god and will say unheard-of things against the God of gods" (verse 36b).

This is very similar to what the apostle Paul says in his second letter to the Thessalonians:

> Don't let anyone deceive you in any way, for [Jesus' return] will not come until ... the man of lawlessness is revealed, the man doomed to destruction. He will oppose and will exalt

himself over everything that is called God or is worshiped, so that he sets himself up in God's temple, proclaiming himself to be God (2 Thessalonians 2:3–4).

As a Pharisee, or religious leader among the Jews, Paul was extremely educated in the writings of the Old Testament. Paul loved to quote from its texts when engaging his audience. There is no other place in Scripture where the wording in this passage is found except chapter 11 of the book of Daniel. Thus, Paul is placing this text and its events specifically at *the time of the end* as stated in Daniel 11:40. It is also worth noting that Paul's writings came long after the demise of Antiochus IV Epiphanes.

"He will show no regard for the gods of his ancestors … nor will he regard any god, but will exalt himself above them all" (verse 37).

When Antiochus desecrated the temple in Jerusalem, he erected an altar to the Greek god Zeus, upon which he sacrificed a pig, adding insult to injury for the Jews. Yet the final antichrist will demand that he alone be worshiped as the one and only true god.

Let us now consider what the remainder of the text in Daniel chapter 11 indicates about this final king in Daniel's vision *"at the time of the end"* (verse 40).

- After additional conflicts, this king will enter *the Beautiful Land* (likely Israel) and will wage war with Egypt and some of its neighbors (verses 40–43).
- *"But reports from the east and the north"* (perhaps of resistance armies) will cause him to *"set out in a great rage to destroy and annihilate many"* (verse 44).
- *"He will pitch his royal tents between the* [sea and] *the beautiful holy mountain."* This likely refers to the Mediterranean Sea and Jerusalem or the Temple

Mount. *"Yet he will come to his end, and no one will help him"* (verse 45).

If the two sentences of verse 45 above are sequentially linked, and this final king is to meet his *end* somewhere between the Mediterranean Sea and Jerusalem, this also is not applicable to Antiochus IV Epiphanes. Antiochus is said to have died in Persia (modern Iran) in 164 BC during a relatively minor conflict.

Daniel chapter 12 picks up where chapter 11 ends and begins with:

"At that time."

Therefore what follows also occurs *"at the time of the end"* (Daniel 11:40a).

Continuing with the text in Daniel chapter 12:

"At that time Michael, the great prince who protects your people, will arise" (verse 1a).

The archangel Michael, whom God has assigned to watch over the Jewish people, will play a predominant role in the things to come (Jude 1:9, Revelation 12:7).

"There will be a time of distress such as has not happened from the beginning of nations until then" (verse 1b).

This is very similar to what Jesus foretold in His Olivet Discourse.

*"For then there will be **great tribulation**, such as has not been from the beginning of the world until now, no, and never will be"* (Matthew 24:21).

From the end of Daniel 12:1 through the remainder of the chapter, one can only speculate what its true meaning might be. The messenger tells Daniel about deliverance and multitudes being awakened from the dust of the earth, *"some to everlasting life, and others to shame and everlasting contempt"* (verse 2). The messenger also states that the *"wise will shine like the brightness of the heavens, and those who lead many to righteousness, like the stars for ever and ever"* (verse 3). Then *"the man clothed in linen"* (verses 6 and 7) says to Daniel, *"Go your way, Daniel, because the words are rolled up and sealed until the time of the end. Many will be purified, made spotless and refined, but the wicked will continue to be wicked. None of the wicked will understand, but those who are wise will understand"* (verses 4 and 9–10).

As *the time of the end* draws nearer, speculation will shift to greater clarity. One thing is certain: those who are wisely and prudently watching will understand.

Let us consider some of the remaining points mentioned in Daniel 12.

Then I, Daniel, looked, and there before me stood two others, one on this bank of the river and one on the opposite bank. One of them said to the man clothed in linen, who was above the waters of the river, "How long will it be before these astonishing things are fulfilled?" The man clothed in linen, who was above the waters of the river, lifted his right hand and his left hand toward heaven, and I heard him swear by him who lives forever, saying, "It will be for a time, times and half a time. When the power of the holy people has been finally broken, all these things will be completed" (verses 5–7).

Once again, as we discovered in our study of Daniel chapter 9, we have an indication of a period of three and a half biblical years comprising 360 days each. You will find this specific wording also in Daniel 7:25 and Revelation 12:14. You will also discover the equivalent timeframe of 1,260 days mentioned in Revelation 11:3 and 12:6, as well as a corresponding period of 42 months in Revelation 11:2. As you dig deeper into end-time events, you will begin to connect more pieces of the puzzle that reveal the amazing things yet to come during *the time of the end.*

But *the man clothed in linen* has some additional measurements of time to share with Daniel:

"*From the time that the daily sacrifice is abolished and the abomination that causes desolation is set up, there will be 1,290 days. Blessed is the one who waits for and reaches the end of the 1,335 days*" (verses 11–12).

The first period, 1,290 days, is 30 days longer than the aforementioned 1,260 days that biblically comprises *a time, times and half a time*. The second measurement of 1,335 days is 75 days beyond this, and even 45 days beyond the 1,290 days. What do they mean? There is a lot of speculation out there, some of which is quite intriguing. Still, it is only speculation at this point. All we can do for now is be faithful with what we do know while we wait for further clarification as God sees fit to reveal it.

Although there are things that will only be understood at the time appointed, you can put into practice right now everything you have learned from our study. Start assembling the puzzle as far as you can. You have enough information in hand to begin developing a well-formulated outline of end-time events on your own. Moving forward, you can continue adding details as you gain further insight from your personal research.

Let us reexamine the foundational principles we have covered in our study that help us learn how to accurately study God's Word. We should:

- Eliminate unwitting filters caused by either our own preconceived ideas about God or any other outside influences.
- Accept certain fundamental beliefs about God and His sovereign ability to communicate His will and plan for all humanity via Scripture.

- Choose the most accurate hermeneutic or method of Bible interpretation.

Next, let us briefly summarize what we have studied.

- We began with Jesus' Olivet Discourse as recounted in Matthew, Mark, and Luke, along with supporting Scriptures from both the Old Testament and the New Testament.
- Based on Jesus' admonition to refer to the writings of Daniel for clarification on the ***abomination of desolation*** (Matthew 24:15), we took a rather in-depth look at one of Daniel's visions in Daniel chapter 9.
- We took a brief look at Daniel chapters 10 through 12 as Daniel's final vision contained in these chapters also makes reference to the ***abomination that causes desolation*** (Daniel 11:31).

In a nutshell, this is what we hopefully have learned from our study:

- Jesus' Olivet Discourse gives us a clearly defined sequential outline of events preceding and surrounding His second coming.
- Jesus' instruction to refer to the writings of Daniel for further clarification concerning the ***abomination of desolation*** is meant to help us discover, among other things, a more specific timeline of events just before His return. If we carefully and diligently watch for the signs He has given, we will not be caught off guard and unprepared for His return. By linking the ***abomination of desolation*** with His physical return, Jesus also makes it clear that the ultimate fulfillment

of this event, as described in the writings of Daniel, has not yet happened but will only occur at *the time of the end.*

Now let us put this into a larger perspective for review.

First, the sequence of events as outlined by Jesus in His Olivet Discourse (taken from **Chapter 5** of this study):

INITIALLY: A gradual increase in:

- False Christianity.
- *Wars and rumors of wars.*
- *Famines and earthquakes.*
- Persecution and death for those that truly believe in Jesus.
- Rejection of the Christian faith and resultant betrayal.
- *Love of many* growing cold.

And **WHEN**:

- The temple at Jerusalem is desecrated by the ***abomination of desolation.***
  (Read in the book of Daniel for further information.)

THEN:

- Comes unparalleled *tribulation* on Earth.
- Do not believe anyone stating they know where Christ is.
- *False christs and false prophets* will come performing miraculous signs and wonders who could *lead astray, if possible, even the elect.*
- It will be obvious when the Son of Man comes.

Immediately **AFTER** this unequaled *tribulation*:

- *The sun will be darkened.*
- *The moon will not give its light.*
- *The stars will fall from the sky.*
- *The powers of the heavens will be shaken.*
- These events signal the Day of the Lord and His judgment.

AT THE SAME TIME:

- The sign of the Son of Man will appear in the sky *as lightning that comes from the east is visible even in the west.*
- All nations will mourn and *see the Son of Man coming on the clouds of the sky with power and great glory.*
- The Son of Man will *send out His angels with a loud trumpet call* and gather His elect from the four winds of heaven and Earth.

Second, while Jesus' Olivet Discourse gives us an important sequential outline of events, He refers us to the writings of Daniel for additional information concerning the ***abomination of desolation***. This begins to give us a clearer timeline of events preceding and surrounding Jesus' return.

- Jesus places the final fulfillment of this event before an unprecedented *tribulation* period on Earth. According to Daniel 9, the ultimate fulfillment of this ***abomination of desolation*** appears to occur in the middle of the last seven years of Daniel's *seventy sevens* prophecy, culminating with the end of sin and

the dawn of *everlasting righteousness* (Daniel 9:24). This only seems possible with Jesus' return.
- We also know from Daniel's *seventy sevens* vision that what initiates this last seven-year period is some sort of *covenant* with *many* (Daniel 9:27). Daniel chapter 11 seems to indicate that this will be a *holy* covenant (Daniel 11:28).
- In summary, the additional information we appear to have as a result of Jesus' admonition to refer to the writings of Daniel to "fill in the blanks," especially Daniel chapters 9 and 11, is this:
  - There is a distinct seven-year period preceding Jesus' return.
  - This seven-year period begins with a major *covenant* that the final *ruler* (ultimate antichrist) is a major part of.
  - Halfway into this seven-year period, this final ruler breaks the *covenant*, sets up an **abomination of desolation**, and declares himself to be a god above all gods. According to Jesus, this initiates the greatest *tribulation* period the world has ever known (Matthew 24:15–21).
  - Directly after this **great tribulation**, Jesus returns.

From our study of Jesus' Olivet Discourse it seems we have an outline of events preceding and surrounding His second coming. From our study of the writings of Daniel, particularly Daniel chapter 9, it seems we also have a timeline of events during the last seven years directly prior to Jesus' return. Do you see it differently? If so, why?

Remember, this study is not meant to establish your endtime doctrine or belief system, though I do hope the commentary has been compelling. The goal from the beginning has been to challenge you, to help you see that research on such matters is not only possible but essential for a true Christ follower. My only warning to you, as I mentioned earlier, is that whatever you decide to accept concerning end-time theology does not lead you into thinking that there is an easy escape. There would seem to be no reason to *watch* if it did not matter (Matthew 25:13).

What are we to gain from our study of Daniel's final vision? As also suggested in our study of Daniel chapter 9, it would be wise to keep a close eye on any *ruler* from the Middle East or its neighbors that begins to show movements similar to those envisioned by Daniel about this final king. Some of the things to look for would include:

- An emerging ruler from the Middle East, or surrounding areas, who acts and moves in ways similar to those described in Daniel 11:21–45.
- A major pact or covenant, one possibly dealing with peace in the Middle East.
- A rebuilding of the Jewish temple in Jerusalem.

If what is stated in Daniel chapter 9 about the last *seven* of Daniel's *seventy sevens* vision is indeed an outline of the last seven years of current world history, the time directly prior to Jesus' return, then once this *covenant* is broken, there will be no time left to make preparations for yourself or anyone else. **Great tribulation** will be upon Earth, particularly toward those who oppose this final antichrist ruler. In short, the signing of this covenant would seem to give those who are diligently watching three and a half years to prepare for the ensuing chaos. We may not know the day or hour of Jesus' return, but He has most definitely given us some serious signs to look for so that His coming does not catch us by surprise *like a thief in the night* (1 Thessalonians 5:4, Revelation 16:15).

It is important to know that this final antichrist ruler, empowered by Satan, will eventually be destroyed at Jesus' return. Nonetheless, for a time he will unleash an unprecedented reign of terror upon all who oppose him. This is why, in Jesus' incredibly merciful love, He encourages us to heed His words of warning to keep watch—and prepare.

Consider once more the apostle Paul's admonition to the church at Thessalonica.

Now concerning the coming of our Lord Jesus Christ and our being gathered together to him, we ask you, brothers, not to be quickly shaken in mind or alarmed, either by a spirit or a spoken word, or a letter seeming to be from us, to the effect that the day of the Lord has come. Let no one deceive you in any way. For that day will not come, unless the rebellion comes first, and the man of lawlessness is revealed, the son of destruction, who opposes and exalts himself against every so-called god or object of worship, so that he takes his seat in the temple of God, proclaiming himself to be God. Do you not remember that when I was still with you I told you these things? And you know what is restraining him now so that he may be revealed in his time. For the mystery of lawlessness is already at work. Only he who now restrains it will do so until he is out of the way. And then the lawless one will be revealed, whom the Lord Jesus will kill with the breath of his mouth and bring to nothing by the appearance of his coming. The coming of the lawless one is by the activity of Satan with all power and false signs and wonders, and with all wicked deception for those who are perishing, because they refused to love the truth and so be saved. Therefore God sends them a strong delusion, so that they may believe what is false, in order that all may be condemned who did not believe the truth but had pleasure in unrighteousness (2 Thessalonians 2:1–12).

This brings us to the close of our study of Jesus' Olivet Discourse, though hopefully not yours. There is certainly much more to be gleaned from Scripture about the end times, particularly from the books of Daniel and Revelation. I hope you have found within these pages some valuable tools that can be of help to you during your own continued research.

We have focused on Jesus' return and the coming judgment. For those that anxiously await His arrival, this will be no surprise or unnecessary burden. Yet for those who fear His judgment, it may well bring a measure of anxiety. For the former there is light—brilliant light—at the end of this tunnel.

But we impart a secret and hidden wisdom of God, which God decreed before the ages for our glory. None of the rulers of this age understood this, for if they had, they would not have crucified the Lord of glory. But, as it is written,

"What no eye has seen, nor ear heard, nor the heart of man imagined, what God has prepared for those who love him"—these things God has revealed to us through the Spirit. For the Spirit searches everything, even the depths of God (1 Corinthians 2:7–10).

In the passage above, the apostle Paul is quoting from the writings of the Old Testament prophet Isaiah, chapter 64. Isaiah was one among many *people of old* who knew what was coming. These Old Testament saints

all died in faith, not having received the things promised, but having seen them and greeted them from afar, and having acknowledged that they were strangers and exiles on the earth. For people who speak thus make it clear that they are seeking a homeland. If they had been thinking of that land from which they had gone out, they would have had opportunity to return. But as it is, they desire a better country, that is, a heavenly one. Therefore God is not ashamed to be called their God, for he has prepared for them a city (Hebrews 11:13–16).

What is this *better country, that is, a heavenly one* that God has prepared *for those who love Him*? What will it be like? What lies ahead, beyond current world history?

The 13th and final chapter is a compilation of verses taken directly from Scripture describing some of the absolutely amazing and wonderful things that God has in store for those He knows and calls His own.

It is simply A Matter Of When

CHAPTER 13

THE MOUNTAIN OF THE LORD, A THOUSAND-YEAR REIGN, AND THE NEW HEAVENS AND NEW EARTH

THE THINGS THE LORD HAS PREPARED FOR THOSE WHO LOVE HIM—BUT ARE THEY LITERAL OR SYMBOLIC?

According to what we have read in Scripture, Jesus' return initiates a series of events that ultimately establishes His rule and reign on Earth forever. Now consider the vision God gave to Nebuchadnezzar, king of Babylon, which the prophet Daniel interpreted by the power of God's Spirit (circa 605–602 BC). This is a study all its own, but I will add some basic explanation in parentheses for clarity. (All verses quoted throughout this chapter are taken from the ESV.)

"*You saw, O king* [Nebuchadnezzar]*, and behold, a great image* [representing the kingdoms of the world from the time of Daniel to the end of our current age]. *This image, mighty and of exceeding brightness, stood before you, and its appearance was frightening. The head of this image was of fine gold* [Babylon], *its chest and arms of silver* [Medo-Persia], *its middle and thighs of bronze* [Greece], *its legs of iron* [Rome], *its feet partly of iron and partly of clay* [post-Roman governments representing a mixture of everything between dictatorships and democracies]. *As you looked, a stone was cut out by no human hand, and it struck the image on its feet of iron and clay, and broke them in pieces. Then the iron, the clay, the bronze, the silver, and the gold, all together were broken in pieces, and became like the chaff of the summer threshing floors; and the wind carried them away, so that not a trace of them could be found. But the stone that struck the image became a great mountain and filled the whole earth.... And in the days of those kings* [represented by feet partly of iron and partly of clay] **the God of heaven will set up a kingdom that shall never be destroyed, nor shall the kingdom be left to another people. It shall break in pieces all these kingdoms and bring them to an end, and it shall stand forever**, *just as you saw that a stone was cut from a mountain by no human hand, and that it broke in pieces the iron, the bronze, the clay, the silver, and the gold"* (Daniel 2:31–35, 44–45a; emphasis added).

What is this *stone* that *became a great mountain filling the whole earth*? Using Scripture to interpret Scripture, consider the following:

> *Jesus said to them, "Have you never read in the Scriptures: 'The stone that the builders rejected has become the cornerstone; this was the Lord's doing, and it is marvelous in our eyes?"* (Matthew 21:42, quoting Psalm 118:22–23)
>
> *This Jesus is the stone that was rejected by you, the builders, which has become the cornerstone* (Acts 4:11).

> *So then you are no longer strangers and aliens, but you are fellow citizens with the saints and members of the household of God, built on the foundation of the apostles and prophets, Christ Jesus himself being the cornerstone, in whom the whole structure, being joined together, grows into a holy temple in the Lord* (Ephesians 2:19–21).
>
> *So the honor is for you who believe, but for those who do not believe, "The stone that the builders rejected has become the cornerstone"* (1 Peter 2:7).

It would seem that Jesus, conceived by the Holy Spirit rather than *human hand* (Luke 1:26–35), is this stone whose kingdom will replace the fallen kingdoms of this world and fill *the whole earth … never be destroyed,… and it shall stand forever.*

There are some scholars who believe we are already living under Jesus' rule from the heavenly realms, even though there is nothing within the context of the passage suggesting that this vision shifts from describing literal kingdoms on Earth to describing a symbolic or spiritual kingdom at the end.

Consider these additional writings from the Old Testament prophets Isaiah and Micah about *the mountain of the house of the Lord.*

> *The word that Isaiah the son of Amoz saw concerning Judah and Jerusalem. It shall come to pass **in the latter days** that **the mountain of the house of the Lord shall be established as the highest of the mountains**, and shall be lifted up above the hills; and all the nations shall flow to it, and many peoples shall come, and say: "Come, let us go up to the mountain of the Lord, to the house of the God of Jacob, that he may teach us his ways and that we may walk in his paths." For out of Zion shall go the law, and the word of the Lord from Jerusalem. He shall judge between the nations, and shall decide disputes for many peoples; and **they shall beat their swords into plowshares, and their spears into pruning hooks; nation shall not lift up sword**

against nation, neither shall they learn war anymore. O house of Jacob, come, let us walk in the light of the Lord (Isaiah 2:1–5; emphasis added).

It shall come to pass **in the latter days** that **the mountain of the house of the Lord shall be established as the highest of the mountains,** *and it shall be lifted up above the hills; and peoples shall flow to it, and many nations shall come, and say: "Come, let us go up to the mountain of the Lord, to the house of the God of Jacob, that he may teach us his ways and that we may walk in his paths." For out of Zion shall go forth the law, and the word of the Lord from Jerusalem. He shall judge between many peoples, and shall decide disputes for strong nations far away; and* **they shall beat their swords into plowshares, and their spears into pruning hooks; nation shall not lift up sword against nation, neither shall they learn war anymore**; *but they shall sit every man under his vine and under his fig tree, and no one shall make them afraid, for the mouth of the Lord of hosts has spoken. For all the peoples walk each in the name of its god, but we will walk in the name of the Lord our God forever and ever.* **In that day, declares the Lord, I will assemble the lame and gather those who have been driven away and those whom I have afflicted; and the lame I will make the remnant, and those who were cast off, a strong nation; and the Lord will reign over them in Mount Zion from this time forth and forevermore** (Micah 4:1–7; emphasis added).

The wolf shall dwell with the lamb, and the leopard shall lie down with the young goat, and the calf and the lion and the fattened calf together; and a little child shall lead them. The cow and the bear shall graze; their young shall lie down together; and the lion shall eat straw like the ox. The nursing child shall play over the hole of the cobra, and the weaned child shall put his hand on the adder's den. ***They shall not hurt or destroy in all my holy mountain; for the earth shall be full of the knowledge of the Lord as the waters cover the sea*** (Isaiah 11:6–9; emphasis added).

Once again, there is no indication in the context that these passages should be understood other than literally. What, then, do we see in these Scriptures? Amongst many things, there is no more war, nothing that will *hurt or destroy in all* [His] *holy mountain*. This alone will be a welcome change—and yet it is only the beginning.

As mentioned earlier in our study, controversies surrounding the end times are not exclusive to either the Olivet Discourse or any of the other passages we have examined. With added detail comes the potential for increased misinterpretation. For example, the apostle Peter mentions in one of his letters to the churches *that with the Lord one day is as a thousand years, and a thousand years as one day.*

This is now the second letter that I am writing to you, beloved. In both of them I am stirring up your sincere mind by way of reminder, that you should remember the predictions of the holy prophets and the commandment of the Lord and Savior through your apostles, knowing this first of all, that ***scoffers will come in the last days with scoffing, following their own sinful desires****. They will say, "Where is the promise of his coming? For ever since the fathers fell asleep, all things are continuing as they were from the beginning of creation." For they deliberately overlook this fact, that the heavens existed long ago, and the earth was formed out of water and through water by the word of God, and that by means of these the world that then existed was deluged with water and perished. But by the same word the heavens and earth that now exist are stored up for fire, being kept until the day of judgment and destruction of the ungodly.*

It is Simply A Matter Of When

*But do not overlook this one fact, beloved, that **with the Lord one day is as a thousand years, and a thousand years as one day**. The Lord is not slow to fulfill his promise as some count slowness, but is patient toward you, not wishing that any should perish, but that all should reach repentance. But the day of the Lord will come **like a thief**, and then the heavens will pass away with a roar, and the heavenly bodies will be burned up and dissolved, and the earth and the works that are done on it will be exposed* (2 Peter 3:1–10; emphasis added).

In context, Peter is reminding us that God lives in the spiritual realm and is not bound, as we are, by the constraints of time. Though we may be tempted to feel that God is slow in moving His plan forward, God always sees the big picture and is accomplishing His will with absolute perfection. Many scholars have tried to use this *thousand years as a day* to minimize the relevance of some specific time periods given in Scripture, relegating them to mere symbolism. This can be dangerous.

One such passage concerns the millennial period of Revelation chapter 20. God knows we live in the dimension of time, and therefore He speaks to us using units of time so we can understand. As we saw with Daniel's *seventy sevens* vision, God revealed to Daniel the exact and literal timing of Jesus' death. Face value hermeneutics teaches that unless the passage suggests otherwise, we should accept what is written as indicated by the context.

Let us look at Revelation chapter 20.

*Then I saw an angel coming down from heaven, holding in his hand the key to the bottomless pit and a great chain. And he seized the dragon, that ancient serpent, who is the devil and Satan, and bound him for a **thousand years**, and threw him into the pit, and shut it and sealed it over him,* *so that he might not deceive the nations any longer, until the **thousand years** were ended. After that he must be released for a little while.*

*Then I saw thrones, and seated on them were those to whom the authority to judge was committed. Also I saw the souls of those who had been beheaded for the testimony of Jesus and for the word of God, and those who had not worshiped the beast or its image and had not received its mark on their foreheads or their hands. They came to life and reigned with Christ for a **thousand years**. The rest of the dead did not come to life until the **thousand years** were ended. This is the first resurrection. Blessed and holy is the one who shares in the first resurrection! Over such the second death has no power, but they will be priests of God and of Christ, and they will reign with him for a **thousand years**.*

*And when the **thousand years** are ended, Satan will be released from his prison and will come out to deceive the nations that are at the four corners of the earth, Gog and Magog, to gather them for battle; their number is like the sand of the sea. And they marched up over the broad plain of the earth and surrounded the camp of the saints and the beloved city, but fire came down from heaven and consumed them, and the devil who had deceived them was thrown into the lake of fire and sulfur where the beast and the false prophet were, and they will be tormented day and night forever and ever.*

Then I saw a great white throne and him who was seated on it. From his presence earth and sky fled away, and no place was found for them. And I saw the dead, great and small, standing before the throne, and books were opened. Then another book was opened, which is the book of life. And the dead were judged by what was written in the books, according to what they had done. And the sea gave up the *dead who were in it, Death and Hades gave up the dead who were in them, and they were judged, each one of them, according to what they had done. Then Death and Hades were thrown into the lake of fire. This is the second death, the lake of fire. And **if anyone's name was not found written in the book of life, he was thrown into the lake of fire*** (Revelation 20; emphasis added).

In this relatively short chapter, a period of a *thousand years* is mentioned six times. Is such repetition deliberate? What do you think? Does this passage of Scripture seem too fantastic to be taken literally? Will those gathered by Jesus at His coming actually rule and reign with Him for *a thousand years* over those who survive God's judgment? (Matthew 24:31) Is this just too surreal to be—well—real?

I would suggest serious consideration of the following: Which part of God's story is not outright over-the-top fantastic? Creation? How about the flood? Then there was Moses leading the Children of Israel out of Egypt through the Red Sea with pillars of smoke and fire leading them around the wilderness. Was that too amazing to be taken literally? What about Samson's exploits, or those of Elijah or Elisha? Where do we draw the line? It is one thing to read about someone being crucified on a cross, but then being raised from the dead after three days along with sightings of angels and the dead walking around the holy city after vacating their tombs? (Matthew 27:52–53) Where does fantastic begin or end with God's story?

Which part of the context in Revelation chapter 20 would lead us to believe that we should understand this millennial period as anything other than literal? Whereas there is obvious symbolism in much of prophetic Scripture, such as with various beasts and images mentioned in Daniel and other parts of Revelation, where is it apparent here? Peter warns of scoffers in the last days *following their own sinful desires* rather than simply believing the Word of God.

Let us continue reading what Peter had to say to the churches concerning *the last days* in his second letter.

> *Since all these things are thus to be dissolved, what sort of people ought you to be in lives of holiness and godliness, waiting for and hastening the coming of the day of God, because of which the heavens will be set on fire and dissolved, and the heavenly bodies will melt as they burn!* **But according to his promise we are waiting for new heavens and a new earth in which righteousness dwells.**
>
> *Therefore, beloved, since you are waiting for these, be diligent to be found by him without spot or blemish, and at peace. And count the patience of our Lord as salvation, just as our beloved brother Paul also wrote to you according to the wisdom given him, as he does in all his letters when he speaks in them of these matters. There are some things in them that are hard to understand, which the ignorant and unstable twist to their own destruction, as they do the other Scriptures. You therefore, beloved, knowing this beforehand,* **take care that you are not carried away with the error of lawless people and lose your own stability**. *But grow in the grace and knowledge of our Lord and Savior Jesus Christ. To him be the glory both now and to the day of eternity. Amen* (2 Peter 3:11–18; emphasis added).

Peter not only warned of *scoffers* and *lawless people* attempting to lead the church astray, but he also encouraged the church with the promise of the *new heavens and new earth* to come.

God gave the prophet Isaiah and the apostle John additional perspective concerning this new world.

> "For behold, I create new heavens and a new earth, and the former things shall not be remembered or come into mind. But be glad and rejoice forever in that which I create;

for behold, I create Jerusalem to be a joy, and her people to be a gladness. I will rejoice in Jerusalem and be glad in my people; **no more shall be heard in it the sound of weeping and the cry of distress.**

"No more shall there be in it an infant who lives but a few days, or an old man who does not fill out his days, for the young man shall die a hundred years old, and the sinner a hundred years old shall be accursed.

"They shall build houses and inhabit them; they shall plant vineyards and eat their fruit. They shall not build and another inhabit; they shall not plant and another eat; for like the days of a tree shall the days of my people be, and my chosen shall long enjoy the work of their hands.

"They shall not labor in vain or bear children for calamity, for they shall be the offspring of the blessed of the Lord, and their descendants with them.

"Before they call I will answer; while they are yet speaking I will hear.

"The wolf and the lamb shall graze together; the lion shall eat straw like the ox, and dust shall be the serpent's food. **They shall not hurt or destroy in all my holy mountain" says the Lord** (Isaiah 65:17–25; emphasis added).

Then I saw a new heaven and a new earth, for the first heaven and the first earth had passed away, and the sea was no more. And I saw the holy city, new Jerusalem, coming down out of heaven from God, prepared as a bride adorned for her husband. And I heard a loud voice from the throne saying, "Behold, the dwelling place of God is with man. He will dwell with them, and they will be his people, and God himself will be with them as their God. **He will wipe away every tear from their eyes, and death shall be no more, neither shall there be mourning, nor crying, nor pain anymore, for the former things have passed away."**

And he who was seated on the throne said, "Behold, I am making all things new." Also he said, "Write this down, for these words are trustworthy and true." And he said to me, "It is done! I am the Alpha and the Omega, the beginning and the end. To the thirsty I will give from the spring of the water of life without payment. The one who conquers will have this heritage, and I will be his God and he will be my son. But as for the cowardly, the faithless, the detestable, as for murderers, the sexually immoral, sorcerers, idolaters, and all liars, their portion will be in the lake that burns with fire and sulfur, which is the second death."

Then came one of the seven angels who had the seven bowls full of the seven last plagues and spoke to me, saying, "Come, I will show you the Bride, the wife of the Lamb." And he carried me away in the Spirit to a great, high mountain, and showed me the holy city Jerusalem coming down out of heaven from God, having the glory of God, its radiance like a most rare jewel, like a jasper, clear as crystal. It had a great, high wall, with twelve gates, and at the gates twelve angels, and on the gates the names of the twelve tribes of the sons of Israel were inscribed—on the east three gates, on the north three gates, on the south three gates, and on the west three gates. And the wall of the city had twelve foundations, and on them were the twelve names of the twelve apostles of the Lamb.

And the one who spoke with me had a measuring rod of gold to measure the city and its gates and walls. The city lies foursquare, its length the same as its width. And he measured the city with his rod, 12,000 stadia. Its length and width and height are equal. He also measured its wall, 144 cubits by human measurement, which is also an angel's measurement. The wall was built of jasper, while the city was pure gold, like clear glass. The foundations of the wall of the city were adorned with every kind of jewel. The first was jasper, the second sapphire, the third agate, the fourth emerald, the fifth onyx, the sixth carnelian, the seventh chrysolite, the eighth beryl, the ninth topaz, the tenth chrysoprase, the eleventh jacinth, the twelfth amethyst. And the twelve gates were twelve pearls, each of the gates made of a single pearl, and the street of the city was pure gold, like transparent glass.

And I saw no temple in the city, for its temple is the Lord God the Almighty and the Lamb. And the city has no need of sun or moon to shine on it, for the glory of God gives it light, and its lamp is the Lamb. By its light will the nations walk, and the kings of the earth will bring their glory into it, and its gates will never be shut by day—and there will be no night there. They will bring into it the glory and the honor of the nations. But nothing unclean will ever enter it, nor anyone who does what is detestable or false, but only those who are written in the Lamb's book of life (Revelation 21; emphasis added).

Is it all literal, symbolic—or a combination of both? If any of it is symbolic, the debate could potentially be endless as to what it really means. But if it is literally going to happen, just as written, it is more than something to look forward to. It is the light at the end of a tunnel that leads not to the end but rather to the beginning of an eternity where the best just keeps getting better and better at every turn.

Scripture only gives us a small glimpse into this incredible future with God. All we know is that it is coming, and those who are God's people will enjoy it forever.

Is any of this difficult for you to grasp or comprehend? Don't worry. You are not alone. Some of the apostles also had questions. During their final Passover feast together, Jesus told them:

"Let not your hearts be troubled. Believe in God; believe also in me. In my Father's house are many rooms. If it were not so, would I have told you that I go to prepare a place

for you? And if I go and prepare a place for you, I will come again and will take you to myself, that where I am you may be also. And you know the way to where I am going." Thomas said to him, "Lord, we do not know where you are going. How can we know the way?" Jesus said to him, "I am the way, and the truth, and the life. No one comes to the Father except through me" (John 14:1–6).

None of us has all the answers. Yet God, in His unfathomable love and mercy, has given us enough information through His Word about Jesus' return, the coming judgment, and the new heavens and new Earth, so that we can be prepared while also being greatly encouraged. Some magnificent and wonderful things await us on a future horizon. Needless to say, you do not want to miss them.

I pray that the analysis contained in this book has accomplished its purpose in your life. For those of you who have held a position about the end times based on what you have been told by others, read elsewhere, or seen in movies, I hope this has helped you reexamine these beliefs based on your own personal study of God's Word. For those that have actually engaged in scriptural research on this topic, I hope it has helped you reassess the basic principles upon which you have built your doctrine. The goal is to successfully eliminate any unwitting filters that might cloud the heart and mind, resulting in misguided conclusions. Finally, for those who have avoided the subject altogether, or have never considered it seriously, I hope this has piqued your interest and equipped you with the tools necessary to begin forming your own sound doctrine.

God wants to make Himself and His plan known to us. He has given us His Word to communicate all that we need to know.

It is there for the taking.

Oh, **taste and see** *that the Lord is good! Blessed is the man who takes refuge in him!* (Psalm 34:8; emphasis added)

It is simply A Matter Of When

www.ingramcontent.com/pod-product-compliance
Lightning Source LLC
Chambersburg PA
CBHW072014110526
44592CB00012B/1304